# THE PAGANISM IN OUR CHRISTIANITY

BY

## ARTHUR WEIGALL

**THE BOOK TREE**
San Diego, California

Originally published
1928
by G. P. Putnam's Sons
New York

ISBN 978-1-58509-328-1

Cover layout and design
by Toni Villalas

Published by
**The Book Tree**
P O Box 16476
San Diego, CA 92176
www.thebooktree.com

We provide fascinating and educational products to help awaken the public to new ideas and
information that would not be available otherwise.
Call 1 (800) 700-8733 for our *FREE BOOK TREE CATALOG*.

# CONTENTS

# CONTENTS

# Introduction

It took three centuries after the death of Jesus for Christianity to become an organized religion, at the Council of Nicea in 325 AD. During this formative time it was difficult for Christianity to compete and survive with the many forms of paganism. In order to succeed and draw new converts into the fold, a number of pagan beliefs and ideas were incorporated into the Christian faith. Today, we do not recognize these pagan features, but the author asserts that they are there and points them out in this well researched book. He reveals how this paganism was brought in, and exactly why it does not belong there. Many long standing pagan festivals were incorporated and given significance—for example, Christianity had abolished the Hebrew Sabbath of Saturday so made Sunday their day of worship, partly because it was the day of the resurrection, but largely because it was the weekly festival of the sun for its main competing rival, Mithraism. Also, December 25th was the birthday of the sun-god, Mithra, so this date was brought in and called Christmas, with full knowledge that Jesus was not born on this day. These are facts. Many more are in this book, covering such things as the influence of pagan gods, the trinity, miraculous occurrences, the composition of the New Testament, the resurrection, the doctrine of atonement, and much more. The author believes Christianity should be what its name infers—based on the teachings of Christ, and not derived from other sources. This book should be read by every interested Christian or student of the history of religions.

Paul Tice

# THE PAGANISM IN OUR CHRISTIANITY

## CHAPTER I

### THE NEED FOR THE RESTATEMENT OF CHRISTIAN THEOLOGY

THE tumult recently aroused in the Church of England by the controversy regarding the proposed alterations in the Prayer Book has reverberated through Christendom; and both in the British Dominions and also in Episcopalian circles in the United States of America, the interest in the questions raised, if not so intense as in England itself, is very marked. In England the lay public, which, on the whole, was quite indifferent to ecclesiastical matters, has suddenly realised in the light of these dissensions how bitter is the warfare which is being waged between the Low Church and the High Church parties, or the Protestants and the Anglo-Catholics, as the two factions are usually termed; but the non-partisan layman, unless he has chanced to be by habit a church-goer, has found it no simple matter to decide which of the two delivers the greater insult to his secular intelligence —the bigoted Evangelical "Fundamentalist," or the strange and subversive Sacramentalist. In this dilemma, therefore, his interest has been directed rather to the matter of keeping the Church as national as possible, in which endeavour he has found himself mainly engaged in attacking practices considered to be of a Roman Catholic character; for the average Englishman has been taught from his youth up, as the eminent Professor George Santayana has said,[1] that any spiritual journey Romewards is tantamount to a renunciation of English nationality.

The Church of England is a State institution, and although a large part of the nation is Nonconformist, this Established Church is supposed to supply the kind of service and teaching most

[1] G. Santayana, *Soliloquies in England.*

4

suitable to the English temperament at large, allowing, however, that degree of latitude necessary in the case of a race of such mixed origin and such varied mentality; and the dominant wish of the English layman, as expressed in Parliament and elsewhere, has been to prevent this national institution passing under the influence of a clerical party not thoroughly representative of traditional English opinion since the Reformation. He has been met, of course, with the threat that the interference of laymen in ecclesiastical affairs will lead to disestablishment, that is to say, to the releasing of the clerical horses from the secular reins; but this threat he has never regarded with any anxiety, for it is obvious that a secession of the Church from the State, against the wishes of Parliament, could only be effected by the clergy's abandonment of the ancient cathedrals and churches in the country and by the building of new places of worship, the historic edifices being national monuments belonging to the English people, too dear sentimentally to them to be handed over to a faction secularly in a minority.

# PAGANISM IN OUR CHRISTIANITY

In England, in fact, the layman finds himself in control of the ecclesiastical situation; but, in making use of his powers, he is mainly concerned with this matter of the national character of the State Church, and he is inclined to give little thought to the intellectual questions involved. The whole fight, however, in its doctrinal aspect, is relatively unimportant, because it is overshadowed by the much more serious fact of the growing indifference of educated people throughout the world to church-going at all. On all sides one hears it said that the dogmas of Christianity can no longer be accepted by the modern mind, there being such a woof of nonsense interwoven across the warp of Christian belief that the intelligent layman must needs weave his own religious fabric. Not merely the English Prayer Book in England, but the whole scheme of Christian theology as taught throughout the world by the various sects and churches, is now under criticism; and though such questions as have agitated the Church of England so violently of late are of great interest to English church-goers and to those who, without actually going to church, are concerned with its doings as a national institution, the really important question to-day is one which is not local nor factional, but is being asked all over the Christian world in all denominations, namely, whether or not the entire creed is obsolete. The fear that Christianity will collapse before the dread tribunal of modern rationality is widespread; and it is perhaps for this reason that the layman in England shrinks from investigating too closely the theological matters involved in this great Prayer Book dispute, and confines himself, as I say, to a somewhat blind opposition to the reintroduction of any foreign practices ejected at the Reformation.

In these chapters I want to bring that lurking fear into the open. As an Englishman I write, of course, with a mental eye chiefly directed toward the Church of England and its twin, the Episcopal Church in the States; and I must confess to a certain prejudice in its favour due to a fact which fairness compels me to admit, namely, that I happen to be respectively the stepson, the grandson, the nephew, and the cousin many times over, of English clergymen. But the present turmoil in Anglican circles does but give point in one country to discussions which are the outcome of modern thought in many lands and amongst persons of many denominations; and I want here to bring Christian theology of all kinds under lay criticism, so that the secular mind may be aided in forming an opinion as to the worth or worthlessness of the Faith. The question as to whether certain practices of the Church of England are "Roman" or not is of but local interest and passing moment: it is the question as to whether Christian theology in general can have the approval of Twentieth Century brains or not that is of real importance.

It will be well, perhaps, here and now to state my own opinion in this matter, so that the trend of my argument may be apparent. Christian theology, I believe, is in part quite acceptable and in part totally unacceptable to the modern mind: such of its doctrines and beliefs as have the genuine authority of the historic Jesus Christ are

8

unassailable and eternal, but those which are based upon the early Christians' interpretation of our Lord's nature and mission are largely untenable. I believe that much of the generally accepted Christian doctrine is derived from pagan sources and not from Jesus Christ at all, a great deal of ecclesiastical Christianity being, indeed, so definitely paganism re-dressed that one might almost speak of it as the last stronghold of the old heathen gods. I believe that the adoration of these ancient gods has never died out, and that in places of Christian worship to-day we still unwittingly maintain it, and solemnly recite the myths of heathendom. Yet the Jesus of History, as distinct from the Jesus of Theology, remains "the way, the truth, and the life"; and I am convinced that concentration upon the historic figure of our Lord and upon His teaching can alone inspire in this Twentieth Century that fervent adherence and service which in former ages could be obtained from the average layman by the expounding of theological dogmas, the threat of hell, and the performance of elaborate rites and ceremonies.

# PAGANISM IN OUR CHRISTIANITY

In saying this I may be accused of attempting to undermine the faith of those who believe, but, on the contrary, my object is to build up the faith of those who do not believe.

The widespread undercurrent of undigested criticism now circulating beneath the outward aspect of Christianity is dangerous in the extreme to the spiritual life of the civilised world, and a bold and rational restatement of the theology of the Faith is urgently called for. The present controversy in regard to the Anglican Prayer Book has revealed the state of religious thought in England; and though this dispute touches only one phase of the wider problem, it is instructive to understand the situation it discloses, which is as follows. The churches of the evangelical and moderate parties, except where the incumbent himself is attractive or provides attractive religious fare, are, on the whole, steadily emptying; but the Anglo-Catholics are managing to infuse some life into their benefices by emphasising the ritualistic and sacramental aspects of their worship, thereby introducing that general effect of colour, drama, mystery, and awe, which is purposely absent in the Protestant service. In doing so, however, they are recalling from limbo the tenets of paganism, and are resuscitating beliefs which can only temporarily galvanise religious fervour, because such beliefs cannot for ever withstand the assault of modern intellectual criticism. Yet so successful is the Anglo-Catholic party in arresting the drift from the Church that the proposed reforms in the Prayer Book have been framed with particular care to legalise certain of their rites and ceremonies, while at the same time setting a limit to the Romeward tendencies of the sect. This licence, however, has aroused the opposition of the Protestants, who, nevertheless, have nothing startling to offer the layman as an inducement to attend their services, and can only rely on the traditional practices and beliefs of the Reformation, many of which are quite unsuited to the modern mind.

Meanwhile, there is a growing body of intellectual clergy and laymen which feels that adherence to the Church is too dearly bought either by the maintenance of obsolete Protestant beliefs or by the introduction of Catholic doctrines and rites which, though they have a dramatic appeal, are of dubious orthodoxy, and which can be seen by any serious student to have their origin in paganism; and these men realise that, no matter which faction be successful in the present dispute, the future life of the Church, and, indeed, of Christianity itself, depends on one thing and one thing alone: namely, the weeding out of such of its teachings as have not the genuine authority of Jesus Christ, and do not show that rationality which makes Him so acceptable to these latter days.

It is here that the local English problem merges with the wider issue. If the things which Christianity throughout the world preaches and the things it does are in accord with modern thought, are credible and acceptable to the critical mind of to-day, and have the authority of the Founder of the Faith, then all is well, and the Christian religion need have no fear of extinction; but if these things are not credible, and neither appeal to modern reason nor find support in the genuine teachings of our Lord, then all the ritualism and sacramentalism on the one hand, or all the evangelical fervour on the other, will not stop the gradual withdrawal of the layman's allegiance to the Churches, and Christianity, as such, is doomed.

The advanced intellectual Christian of the Twentieth Century wishes to have the very creed itself pulled to pieces and rewritten, and he desires to see the removal of all those features which render his Faith open to the criticism that it is heathendom rehabilitated. The old gods, ousted by Jesus, have crept back, and have, so to speak, dug themselves in once more. Their temples being destroyed and their altars forsaken, they have come to church; and there you may find them to-day, receiving, under other names, the worship denied them in their own immemorial forms. Drastic measures are needed to rescue the sublime figure of our Lord from the press of this motley company, and to relieve the original doctrine from the stranglehold of a theology and a habit of religious thought which are to be traced to primitive paganism. The old gods have come to church; and, their presence beginning at long last to be detected, the day will soon arrive when either they or the congregation must leave.

# CHAPTER II

DURING the frank and unbiassed examination of the theology and customs of our Faith which I propose to make, I shall have to question certain dogmas and beliefs the truth of which will be thought by the orthodox to be beyond doubt; and to those who are not familiar with theological criticism it may seem that an attempt is being made to destroy the whole structure of Christianity. My object, however, is, as I have said, precisely the reverse. There is a widespread critical school which, seeing only the old gods grouped about the Christian altar, thinks that Jesus never existed at all, but that His life is a myth invented during the First Century A.D.; and it is with this powerful school that I wish to do battle.

There is no use in defending an untenable

position, and therefore the first thing to be done is to abandon the territory which can be no longer held; but it will gradually be seen that in throwing over certain time-honoured beliefs my purpose is to present a Christian frontage which shall be impregnable. It may be stated as an axiom that the kind of evidence which was required by the man of the First Century A.D. to prove the divinity of Jesus is the very kind which has an opposite effect on the mind of the man of the Twentieth Century; and therefore it is obviously the duty of the Christian scholar to-day to delete from the story of our Lord all that is incredible or repugnant to the modern intelligence, and, so far as is possible, to restore the true facts and the simplicity of the creed dependent upon them.

It is essential that Christianity should be in a position to meet the highest intellectual demands of modern times; and it would show the grossest form of superstition to refrain from free criticism for fear of being thought heretical or blasphemous. It has been truly said by a doughty champion of the Faith[1] that religious knowledge is now neither acquired nor made valid by belief in the supernatural, and that while the thinkers of the First Century found their highest thoughts expressed in terms of the miraculous, we of to-day find ours most easily expressed through the natural and the rational.

If the teachings and the acts of Jesus Christ —and I believe them to be the world's only hope—are to be fully brought to the spiritual aid of modern men and women, they must not be cramped into the mould of the outlook of people of eighteen or nineteen hundred years ago. We have got to release the historic Christ from the confinement of an earlier theological interpretation; for He is eternal, whereas the dogmas of the Christian Church are not. God's revelation is gradual; and no intelligent thinker to-day can possibly adhere entirely to the interpretation placed upon the life and death of Jesus by those who lived shortly after His time, that is to say, in days when the wildest mythological nonsense

[1] Shirley Jackson Case, *The Historicity of Jesus.*

17

was blandly accepted all around them as fact. If we may believe the rather doubtful testimony of the Fourth Gospel, Jesus Himself said: "I have yet many things to say unto you, but ye cannot bear them now: howbeit, when he, the Spirit of truth, is come, he shall guide you into all truth";[1] and these words may well carry the meaning that the understanding of Him was not for the men of His own day. It may not be for us either; but at least we can remove the ancient veil from our eyes and make the attempt to see Him—the Eternal One—in His present aspect as Lord also of the Twentieth Century.

But the constricted Jesus of Christian theology does not belong to modern times: He is dated; He is the product of the early centuries A.D., when men believed in Olympus, and drenched its altars with the blood of sacrificial victims. Ancient magic plays about Him like lightning, and the primitive conception of the supernatural thunders in answer to His behests. He walks upon the waters, ascends into the air, is obeyed

[1] John xvi. 12.

by the tempests, turns water into wine, blasts the fig-tree, multiplies the loaves and fishes, raises the dead. His birth was heralded by signs and wonders; a star appeared in the East; hosts of angels sang in the heavens; the clouds opened at His baptism, and the voice of God echoed over the world; while at His Crucifixion darkness hid the sun, the earth quaked, and the dead came forth from their graves. All these marvels made Him God incarnate to the thinkers of the First Century; all these marvels make Him a conventional myth to those of the Twentieth.

Many of the most erudite critics are convinced that no such person ever lived. Their argument is based primarily upon the fact that ancient mythology is full of stories of incarnate gods who suffered on behalf of mankind, who died, were buried, descended into hell, and rose again from the dead, and by whose redeeming blood the faithful were saved. Many of the recorded incidents of the life of Jesus, they point out, have their parallels in pagan mythology or in early Judaism; and the very story of the Crucifixion seems to be derived[1] from the earlier account of the death of a certain Jesus ben Pandira who was slain and hanged on a tree on the eve of the Passover in the reign of Alexander Jannæus, who lived about a hundred years B.C.[2]

There is evidence, it is suggested, of the cult of a sun-god called Joshua or Jesus in primitive times, whose twelve disciples were the twelve signs of the Zodiac; and just as Jesus Christ with His twelve apostles came to Jerusalem to eat the Paschal lamb, so Joshua crossed the Jordan with his twelve helpers and offered that lamb on the other side, and so the Greek Jason—an identical name[3]—with his twelve retainers went in search of the golden fleece of the lamb.

It is pointed out that there are no contemporary or nearly contemporary references to Jesus in history, with the exception of those in the genuine Epistles of Paul and Peter, where, how-

---

[1] W. B. Smith, *Der Vorchristliche Jesus;* Drews, *The Christ Myth.*

[2] This Jesus is mentioned in the *Talmud, Sanhedrin,* 107 b; *Sota,* 47A.

[3] Josephus, *Antiquities,* 12, v. 1.

ever, His life on earth is hardly mentioned at all, nor anything which really establishes Him as a historic personage. Even Justus of Tiberias, an historian who was born in Galilee itself, only a few years after the death of Jesus, and who wrote the Chronicle of the Jewish Kings and other books, makes no reference to our Lord. The works of Justus are lost, but they were read by Photius, Patriarch of Constantinople, in the Ninth Century, who expresses[1] his surprise at finding no mention of Jesus therein. Pliny the Elder, in his great *Historia Naturalis*, compiled thirty or forty years after the supposed death of Jesus, makes no reference to any of the wonders described in the Gospels; yet he loved the marvellous, and recorded every occurrence of the kind which came under his notice or of which he had read in the two thousand volumes declared to have been consulted by him.

Tacitus, who wrote before A.D. 115, refers[2] to our Lord, and says that He was put to death

[1] *Cod.*, 33 (Migne ed., ciii. col. 65).
[2] *Annal.* xv. 44.

by Pontius Pilate in the reign of Tiberius; but the genuineness of the passage has been questioned.[1]  Josephus, in his *Antiquities of the Jews*,[2] finished in A.D. 93, twice refers to Jesus; but the paragraphs have undoubtedly been tampered with, and many critics think that they are entire forgeries.  Pliny the Younger, in his famous letter to Trajan written about A.D. 112, refers to the early Christians; but the genuineness of this document is, again, sometimes doubted.[3]  And, finally, Suetonius, writing about A.D. 120, twice mentions the sect,[4] and says that they were instigated by a certain *Chrestus;* but this is ambiguous.

The Gospels, as I shall explain in the next chapter, were not written until the last quarter of the First Century and first quarter of the Second Century, and therefore are open to the charge of being fiction.  Personally, however, I am quite certain that, when stripped of their supernatural trappings, and when critically edited, they

[1] Hochart, *De l'authenticité des Annales de Tacite.*
[2] xviii. iii. 3; xx. ix. 1.
[3] G. Brandes, *Jesus, a Myth*, p. 48.
[4] *Claudius*, xxv.; *Nero*, xvi.

place before us with absolutely unmistakable authenticity the historic figure of a young man, the son of a carpenter, who went about the country preaching and healing the sick, who was ultimately regarded by a small group of disciples as the Messiah or Christ, who was crucified as an impostor, and, after being taken down from the cross as dead, was seen alive by many persons. Brief as was the time of His ministry, and meagre and garbled as are the accounts of it which have come down to us, the character of Jesus stands out as the most godlike in history, while His teaching, delivered in the First Century A.D., is such as to satisfy both the demands of the highest intellects, and the aspirations of the most cultured minds, of the Twentieth Century.

But around this historic figure a mass of pagan legends collected, and a great theological structure grew up; and to-day these have to be removed, so that we may get back to the real and credible Jesus. We have to face the fact that the church congregations are dwindling because people are saying—and quite rightly—that many of the dogmas of the Faith are borrowed from paganism, and many of the details of the life of our Lord are too wildly improbable to be accepted in these sober days. But Christianity need not be dismayed, for behind the tottering structure of its theology stands the unassailable figure of the real Jesus; and He is the same yesterday, to-day, and for ever—if only we can break through to Him past the ring of old gods who have surrounded Him.

# CHAPTER III

## THE COMPOSITION OF THE NEW TESTAMENT

BORN and bred as most of us have been in the Christian Faith, it has been usual in the past for us to accept the New Testament as the true basis of the religion, and to regard it as being above criticism, without giving the matter much thought. Thus, if an event or a saying has been quoted from one of the Gospels, we have assumed that it was authentic, and have quite overlooked the fact that the earliest Gospel was not compiled until at least seventy years after the birth of our Lord, while the New Testament as a whole contains material written down at various times over a period of perhaps more than a hundred years, and that, therefore, any such quotation ought first to be dated and textually scrutinised before it is used for historical purposes. No Biblical scholar of any standing to-day, whether he be a

25

clergyman, a minister, or a layman, accepts the entire New Testament as authentic; and all admit that many errors, misunderstandings, and absurdities have crept into the story of Christ's life and other matters. Indeed, it is now generally acknowledged amongst students that the recognition of these mistakes, far from being the act of a heretic, is the first duty of the intelligent Christian.

The time is past when we could give our adherence to beliefs which have no sound historic foundation, and justify ourselves in so doing by saying that the New Testament is the infallible Word of God; for the answer of the critic is simply: "Who says it is?"—to which there is no reply other than a repetition of the statement that such is the Christian belief. Christian proofs must be submitted to the ordinary critical tests applied to other matters; and, indeed, no faith would be worth holding which could not confidently subject the documents on which it was founded to a keener and more penetrating criticism than any bestowed upon other writings.

Let me therefore briefly summarise the results

of the labours of modern scholars in regard to the dates at which the books of the New Testament were written, so that the unprejudiced reader may judge of their historical value or liability to error by considering the length of time which elapsed between the days of Jesus and those of their composition.[1]

The earliest known Christian documents are the Epistles of Paul, who died, it would seem, about the year A.D. 64, and whose first letter was written at least a dozen years before that date, that is to say, some twenty years after the Crucifixion. Some of these Epistles have been regarded as not genuine Pauline writings, but the extreme views of Bauer and others in this regard have found little support; and it is now generally thought that the authenticity of Galatians, I and II Corinthians, and Romans, is unquestionable, and that Philippians and I Thessalonians are

[1] Amongst the extensive literature on this subject mention may be made of the following works:—Moffatt, *Introduction to the Literature of the New Testament;* Burkitt, *Gospel History and its Transmission;* Loisy, *Les évangiles synoptiques;* Giran, *Jesus of Nazareth; The Encyclopædia Britannica* articles.

probably Pauline. Colossians, Ephesians, and II Thessalonians are thought to be more doubtful, though the great critic, Dr. Rashdall, Dean of Carlisle, accepted them with reserve.[1]

Certain critics regard I Thessalonians as the earliest Epistle, and place its date at about A.D. 52 (Lightfoot) or even earlier (Harnack). It is important, however, to notice that nowhere in the Epistles is there any reference to written records of the life of Jesus; and it seems pretty certain, therefore, that nothing in the nature of a Gospel was then in existence—a fact which is not surprising, since His Second Coming and the end of the world were then believed to be imminent.

Papias, Bishop of Hierapolis, who wrote in about the year 140, and who is quoted by Eusebius,[2] says that Mark, the interpreter and follower of Peter, wrote down all that he could remember of the words and acts of Jesus as related by Peter, although he had not himself known Jesus in the flesh. This document is said[3] to have been writ-

---

[1] H. Rashdall, *Idea of Atonement*, p. 84, note.
[2] Eusebius, *Hist. Eccl.* iii. 39.
[3] Irenæus, *Hær.* iii. i. 2.

ten soon after the death of Peter, which is thought to have taken place about the year 64; but the work is now lost in its original form, though the Gospel of St. Mark as we now have it is based upon it, and seems to have assumed more or less its present shape between A.D. 70 and 100, somewhere about A.D. 90 being the most probable date. It should be mentioned, however, that the last twelve verses (xvi. 9–20) are thought to have been written some years later to replace the proper ending, which had got lost.

With the exception of some thirty verses the whole of the Gospel of St. Mark is contained in the Gospels of St. Luke and St. Matthew; but these two latter also contain material thought to have been obtained from some collection of our Lord's sayings and deeds which was not known to the compilers of the Gospel of St. Mark, and which is now referred to by scholars as "Q." This lost work is probably one also mentioned by Bishop Papias, who says that Matthew wrote in the Hebrew language certain sayings of Jesus which each teacher interpreted as best he could.

# PAGANISM IN OUR CHRISTIANITY

The Gospel of St. Luke as we now have it is generally regarded as the next oldest after that of St. Mark; but whether it was written by Luke, "the beloved physician" and fellow-worker with St. Paul, is not known, for the earliest mention of Luke as its author occurs in a statement made by Irenæus about A.D. 180. It has been pointed out that the author of this Gospel seems to have had a knowledge of the *Antiquities of the Jews* by Josephus, and in this case the book cannot be dated earlier than A.D. 93, but if this be not so, it might be dated as early as A.D. 80, though critics usually assign it to about A.D. 100. Its preface mentions the fact that there were then several written accounts of our Lord's life and sayings in existence; for the hope of an immediate Second Coming having by then begun to fade, there was need of a record of His teachings in regard to man's duties on earth.

The Gospel of St. Matthew as it now appears in the New Testament is recognised as being later than that of St. Luke. The first known instance of Matthew's name being attached to it occurs in a reference made to it by Irenæus (A.D. 180); but it was probably compiled anonymously from the lost original work of Mark and from the lost collection of sayings made by Matthew, together with other sources now unknown. Later additions seem to have been made to it throughout the Second Century; but, apart from these, it is generally agreed that it was compiled between A.D. 100 and 110.

These three Gospels, now known as those of St. Mark, St. Luke, and St. Matthew, are called the Synoptic Gospels, owing to the fact that they admit of being regarded as presenting one general view or *synopsis* of the subject. But quite in another category stands the beautiful work now known as the Gospel of St. John. Its date is much disputed: some critics place it as early as A.D. 100, and some as late as A.D. 160, but recent opinion tends rather towards a date of about A.D. 105, though Bishop Papias, writing about A.D. 140, does not mention it, so far as we know from Eusebius, nor is there any indication that Marcion, who also wrote at that date, was acquainted with it. Justin Martyr uses it in his writings dating from A.D. 163 to 167; but he does so with reserve, as though the work were not regarded as authoritative, and, indeed, there is other evidence to show that it was not accepted as authentic even as late as the Third Century. Its author was certainly not John, the disciple of Jesus; but if its early date be accepted, he may have been John the Presbyter, who died about A.D. 100.

The work entitled *The Acts of the Apostles* is thought to have been written in its original form by the author of the Gospel of St. Luke, who may possibly have been Luke himself; and its date may perhaps be as early as A.D. 80; though some critics think that it was not published until after A.D. 100.

The book known as *The Revelation of St. John* is thought to be the work of a student of the same school to which the author of the Gospel of St. John belonged; but it is an earlier book than the Gospel, and was probably written between A.D. 69 and 93. Andreas of Cæsarea states that Bishop Papias knew the work; Justin Martyr accepted it as canonical; Marcion knew it but rejected it; Dionysius of Alexandria (A.D. 255) was doubtful whether to call it spurious or authentic; Jerome, who died in A.D. 420, rejected it; but other Christian writers accepted it, and gradually the opinion became general that it should be received as canonical.

Finally, there are the non-Pauline epistles. Of these the First Epistle of St. Peter is generally thought to be a genuine letter of Peter, written between A.D. 59 and 64; but the Second Epistle of St. Peter is by a later hand, and probably dates from about A.D. 150. The Epistles of St. John are thought to have been written between A.D. 90 and 110; that of St. James between A.D. 95 and 120; and that of St. Jude between A.D. 100 and 150.

Thus, the books of the New Testament may be placed in the following order:—The genuine Pauline Epistles, from A.D. 52 to 64; the first Epistle of St. Peter, from A.D. 59 to 64; Revelation, from A.D. 69 to 93; the Gospel of St. Mark, from A.D. 70 to 100; the Acts, from A.D. 80 to 100; the Epistles of St. John, from A.D. 90 to 110; the Epistle of St. James, from A.D. 95 to 120; the Gospel of St. Luke, about A.D. 100; the Gospel of St. Matthew, from A.D. 100 to 110; the Epistle of St. Jude, from A.D. 100 to 150; the Gospel of St. John, from A.D. 100 to 160; and the Second Epistle of St. Peter, about A.D. 150.

In this Twentieth Century it is astounding to hear Christian people declare that the Bible, and particularly the New Testament, says so-and-so, and that therefore it must be true. Do they not understand that the New Testament is a collection of books of varying credibility put together and accepted as canonical only in the Fourth Century A.D., by clergy having the limited mentality of that very uncritical age? In quoting from the New Testament the above-mentioned dates should always be kept in mind; and in regard to the Gospels it should be remembered that St. Matthew and St. John are the least trustworthy, so many years having elapsed in which errors may have crept in. Nevertheless, when the element of the incredibly supernatural is removed, these canonical books provide us with a literature which is of first-rate historical importance.

# CHAPTER IV

## THE VIRGIN BIRTH

THE orthodox Christian is inclined to lay a greater stress upon the theological aspect of his religion than upon the ethical; that is to say, he is more interested in the worship of Christ as God than in the following of His example as man. It is more pleasing to him to think of our Lord as having been born in a miraculous manner, to the accompaniment of the shouts of the host of heaven, and as having lived a gloriously spectacular life, performing miracles and ministered to by angels, than it is to regard Him as having been, while on earth, simply a man, battling with the same difficulties with which we ourselves have to contend.

This tendency to emphasise His godhead, so that He may be worshipped, rather than to emphasise His manhood, so that He may be followed, was also apparent in early Christian days; for the desire to fall down and adore instead of to stand up and obey is a chronic human weakness. Thus it came about that some sixty years or so after the Crucifixion the story began to be circulated that Jesus had been "conceived by the Holy Ghost," and had had no human father.

One might have supposed that such a belief would have been seen to detract from the value of His exemplary life, for it implied that that life had enjoyed the advantage of being only half mortal, and was therefore no example for mere men, since He had not inherited, as we do, the mortal tendencies and failings of a human mother *and* father. But the point was overlooked; and, indeed, this wish to regard our Lord as having been more than mortal even during His mortal incarnation became, as the centuries passed, so strong that it was found necessary to ascribe a kind of divinity to His earthly mother also, so that He might be considered as altogether non-human.

In 1854 the doctrine of the "Immaculate Conception of the Mother of God," which had been vaguely preached for many centuries, was officially adopted by the Roman Catholic Church as a tenet of the Faith, this having the meaning that the mother of Jesus, from the moment of her conception by her parents, was miraculously free from the taint of Original Sin, and thus remained all her life in a non-human state of sinlessness. This dogma, taken together with the fact that the Church had already canonised her parents as saints, implies that Jesus did not set an imitable example to ordinary men of how a man's life could be lived, for He inherited no parental failings and had no such handicap as that under which we ourselves labour.

This is all to the liking of those who are temperamentally disposed towards worship, and who therefore, as I say, prefer to think of our Lord as God and not as Man: but those to whom His greatest appeal is His heroic manhood would prefer to think, as did the early Christians in the days before Theology took hold of the Faith, that in His incarnation He was simply the son of an obscure carpenter, named Joseph, and of his wife, probably called Mary. I say "probably," in the first place because there is no certainty that the name of the mother of Jesus was Mary, the earliest reference to her under that name being in a possibly interpolated passage in Acts,[1] which book was not written until between fifty and seventy years after the Crucifixion; and, in the second place, because so many gods and semi-divine heroes have mothers whose names are variations of "Mary": Adonis, son of Myrrha; Hermes, the Greek Logos, son of Maia; Cyrus, the son of Mariana or Mandane; Moses, the son of Miriam; Joshua, according to the Chronicle of Tabarí, the son of Miriam; Buddha, the son of Maya; Krishna, the son of Maritala; and so on, until one begins to think that the name of our Lord's mother may have been forgotten and a stock name substituted.

In regard to the Virgin Birth, it is significant that there is no reference to it in the Epistles which form the earliest Christian documents; but,

[1] Acts i. 14.

on the contrary, St. Paul speaks of Jesus as "made of the seed of David according to the flesh,"[1] that is to say, of the seed of Joseph, David's descendant. The earliest Gospel, that of St. Mark, dating between A.D. 70 and 100, does not mention it; nor does the Gospel of St. John, dating from some time not earlier than A.D. 100. The Book of Revelation, written between A.D. 69 and 93, is silent on the subject, though had the Virgin Birth then been an important tenet of the faith it would undoubtedly have figured in the mystical symbolism of that composition. The story appears for the first time in the Gospel of St. Luke, which may have been written as late as A.D. 100; and there we are told that Mary had conceived her child by the Holy Ghost before the consummation of her marriage with Joseph, though it is implied that he believed the baby to be his own son,[2] and that this was the general opinion.[3] In the Gospel of St. Matthew, perhaps ten years later again, the account has developed. Joseph is now

[1] Romans i. 3.
[2] Luke ii. 5, 16, 41.          [3] Luke iii. 23.

said to have been aware that the child was not his, and to have been restrained from divorcing Mary by an angel who came to him in a dream and told him that the baby had been conceived by the Holy Ghost.

It seems clear, therefore, that the story was not known, or at any rate was not accepted, before A.D. 100, that is to say, a whole century after the date of the event it records. But both in St. Matthew and in St. Luke the genealogy of our Lord is given, for the purpose of showing that Jesus was descended from David; for the promised Messiah was to be of the seed of David. These genealogies, however, are traced through Joseph; and if Joseph was not then thought to be the father of Jesus it is difficult to understand why the pedigree was given at all, for there is no suggestion anywhere that Mary was related to Joseph or was also descended from David, nor does she figure in the genealogies. The Syriac version of the Gospels, discovered in 1892,[1] throws more light upon

---

[1] Abbé Houtin, *La Question Biblique*, p. 245; E. Giran, *Jesus of Nazareth*, p. 56.

the subject, for there, at the end of the genealogy, the definite statement is made that "Jacob had a son, Joseph, to whom was betrothed the Virgin Mary; and Joseph had a son, Jesus, called the Christ." It seems, in fact, that we have to deal with a contradiction due to the later insertion of the story of the Virgin Birth beside the earlier story of the descent of Jesus from David through Joseph; and, in this case, we may place its inception somewhere in the Second Century.

The growth of such a story may well be understood, for tales of the births of pagan gods and heroes from the union of a deity with a mortal maiden were common. The famous Egyptian Queen, Hetshepsut, was stated to have been the daughter of the union of the god Amon with her mortal mother; and a similar story regarding the birth of Amenophis III, fully illustrated by sculptures, was to be read and seen by any traveller in Egypt who happened to visit the temple of Amon at Thebes. So also the great Cyrus was said to have been the son of a god by union with a mortal maiden, and this Cyrus was thought by the Jews at one time to be the Messiah.[1] The Egyptian writer, Asclepiades, states that Julius Cæsar was miraculously conceived by Apollo in the womb of his mother when she was in the temple of that god. The famous hero, Perseus, was the son of the god Zeus by a virgin princess named Danae, a fact which caused Justin Martyr, one of the Christian Fathers in the middle of the Second Century, to write: "When I hear that Perseus was begotten of a virgin, I understand that the deceiving serpent (Satan) has counterfeited this,"[2] apparently to excite doubt in regard to the story of the Virgin Birth of Jesus which was then beginning to be believed.

According to one legend, the father of the philosopher Plato was warned in a dream of the child's coming birth, his wife, who was still a virgin, having been divinely fertilised;[3] and Plutarch mentions the common belief that women might conceive at the approach of a spirit or

---

[1] Isaiah xlv. 1.  [2] *Dial. with Trypho*, c. 70.
[3] *Diogenes Laertius*, b. iii., c. i., sec. 1; J. M. Robertson, *Christianity and Mythology*, p. 318, note 6.

divinity. Apollonius of Tyana, the contemporary of Jesus, was likewise said to have been born of the union of a god with his mother, to whom the coming birth was announced somewhat as in the Christian tale. In China the philosophers Fohi and Lao-Kium were both born of virgin mothers; and the Persian Zoroaster was miraculously conceived in the same manner. The mother of the god Attis, according to one legend, was the Virgin Nana; and the Egyptian goddess Neit conceived without union with a male, and brought forth Ra. Herodotus tells us how a ray of light descended on the Sacred Cow of Egypt, which thereupon conceived and brought forth the god Apis. Plutarch, in his book on Isis and Osiris, says that such conceptions occur through the ear; and in mediæval pictures we sometimes see a ray of light descending in like manner into Mary's ear. Tertullian states[1] that our Lord was conceived by a ray of light which thus struck down upon the Virgin.

The story of a miraculous conception having

[1] Tertullian, *Apolog.* xxi.

gained credence in regard to Jesus, it seems that the old Hebrew prophecy in reference to the birth of the Messiah had to be adjusted to it. Both in St. Matthew and St. Luke the prophetic words of Isaiah are referred to: "Behold a virgin shall conceive and bear a son";[1] and the Greek word *parthenos*, usually meaning an actual virgin, is employed. But Isaiah had really used the Hebrew *almah*, which does not necessarily mean a virgin at all;[2] and thus the original tradition did not require the Messiah to be born of a virgin.

But in spite of the circulation of the story of the Virgin Birth nobody paid much attention to it in early times, and the view held by St. Paul[3] that Jesus was the son of Joseph but had been declared the Son of God "through the Spirit of Holiness" was generally accepted. His actual nativity was not celebrated, but the anniversary of His baptism was regarded as the important annual event, because, as Chrysostom says: "It

[1] Isaiah vii. 14.
[2] Compare Joel i. 8, where an *almah's* husband is mentioned.
[3] Rom. i. 4.

44

was not when He was born that He became manifest to all, but when He was baptised." It was widely thought that His divine life only began with His baptism, and as late as about A.D. 450 Pope Leo[1] had to correct some of his bishops for thinking that Jesus was "born of the Holy Ghost" at this baptism; which shows how unimportant the real nativity and the stories regarding it were considered to be.

In view of these facts it seems a pity that the Virgin Birth of Jesus should be insisted upon as an article of the Creed. Some people, it is true, find no difficulty in accepting it, since parthenogenesis, or conception without male fertilisation, is a known fact in the lower animal, if not in the human, world. But other people boggle at it: firstly, because it diminishes the fullness of our Lord's victory over the flesh to suppose that He was only half a human; secondly, because it is sufficient to the idea of His divinity to suppose, as did the early Christians, that the Spirit of God first suffused His personality at the beginning of

[1] 18th Epistle to Bishops of Sicily.

His ministry; thirdly because all the evidence goes to show that the story was not known until a century after His birth; and lastly, because at that time the pagan world was so full of such legends that the early Christians could hardly have escaped their influence.

# CHAPTER V

THE task of removing from the record of the life and ministry of our Lord those events which are incredible, or which seem to have been borrowed from contemporary mythology, is one which may be undertaken without the dread of any adverse consequences upon one's faith, but, on the contrary, with a sense of happiness and relief. Some critics have been worried by these unbelievable incidents into a general agnosticism, and others have employed them with energy as arguments to prove that Jesus never existed at all; and it is, therefore, a matter of profound satisfaction to find that such legends can be discarded without detracting from the supreme value of the Gospel story.

Let us consider, then, what parts of the accounts of our Lord's life may be regarded as historical.

In the first place we have to recognise that nothing is known with certainty about His birth, childhood, and early manhood; for in the earliest Gospel, that of St. Mark, the story opens at the beginning of His ministry, and so it does, too, in the Gospel of St. John. The early years are only recounted in the Gospels of St. Luke and St. Matthew, neither of which dates before A.D. 100; and, even so, the two accounts are essentially different.

In St. Matthew, the parents of Jesus live in Bethlehem,[1] which is in Judæa, about five miles south of Jerusalem, but migrate to Nazareth in Galilee, far north of Jerusalem, after their return from Egypt;[2] but in St. Luke they live in Nazareth,[3] and go to Bethlehem only for the purpose of being taxed.[4] The Gospel of St. Mark, our best authority, speaks of Jesus as "of Nazareth,"[5] but makes no mention at all of Bethlehem. Now, many critics[6] have argued that there was no such place as Nazareth, for, outside the Bible, there is

---

[1] Implied in Matt. ii. 1.    [2] Matt. ii. 23.    [3] Luke i. 26.
[4] Luke ii. 4.    [5] Mark xiv. 67; xvi. 6.
[6] G. Brandes, *Jesus, a Myth*, p. 92.

48

no reference to it as a village either before the Christian era or in the first three centuries A.D., and they suggest that it was a place-name invented, and afterwards attached to an appropriate village, to account for the forgotten origin of the title " Jesus the Nazarite," the real origin of which, they argue, was the Hebrew root-word *n s r*, meaning "to protect," "Jesus the Protector" being, perhaps, the name of an old Hebrew folk-god long before the time of our Lord. The general opinion, however, is that the present village of Nazareth in Galilee was, in fact, the home of Jesus; but there is an equally general doubt that He was born at Bethlehem in Judæa. The Bethlehem story, it is thought, was introduced in order to strengthen the idea that He was the Messiah, for the family of David, of whose seed the Messiah was to be born, sprang from this Bethlehem in Judæa. Actually, however, it is more probable that Jesus was born in a little hamlet still called Bethlehem, close to Nazareth in Galilee.[1] The story of the taking of a census by order of Augustus, which compelled

[1] A. Réville, *Jesus of Nazareth.*

Joseph and Mary to go to Bethlehem in Judæa, is pretty certainly incorrect; for no such census is known to have been made in any year which can be regarded as a likely date of the birth of Jesus, if we assume that He was somewhere about thirty at the beginning of His ministry. It is obviously impossible, also, that citizens should have been obliged to proceed to their ancestral home to be numbered, and, indeed, it is known that all Roman censuses were made at the place of residence of the citizens. Moreover, Galilee was ruled independently by Herod Antipas at the time when Quirinius, or Cyrenius,[1] went to tax Judæa.

In St. Matthew Jesus was born in a house;[2] but in St. Luke He is born in a stable,[3] and in later times this stable is generally represented as being in a cave. The mythological origin of this idea, however, is so obvious that the whole story must be abandoned. Firstly, as regards the cave: the cave shown at Bethlehem as the birthplace of Jesus was actually a rock shrine in which the god Tammuz or Adonis was worshipped, as

[1] Luke ii. 2.       [2] Matt. ii. 11.       [3] Luke ii. 7.

the early Christian Father, Jerome, tells us;[1] and its adoption as the scene of the birth of our Lord was one of those frequent instances of the taking over by Christians of a pagan sacred site. The propriety of this appropriation was increased by the fact that the worship of a god in a cave was a commonplace in paganism: Apollo, Cybele, Demeter, Herakles, Hermes, Mithra and Poseidon were all adored in caves, Hermes, the Greek *Logos*, being actually born of Maia in a cave,[2] and Mithra being "rock-born."

Then, as regards the stable: St. Luke[3] says that when the child was born Mary wrapped Him in swaddling clothes and laid Him in a manger (*phatné*), that is to say a rough trough, like the Greek *liknon*, which was a sort of basket used either for hay or as an actual cradle, somewhat as the manger is represented in Botticelli's picture of the Nativity.[4] The author of the Gospel of St. Luke, however, was here drawing upon Greek mythology; for the god Hermes was wrapped

[1] Epist. lviii., *ad Paulinum.*     [2] *Apollodorus*, book iii., x. 2.
[3] Luke ii. 7.     [4] National Gallery, London.

in swaddling clothes when he was born and was placed in a *liknon*, or manger-basket. So, also, was the god Dionysos,[1] who, in Bithynia, gave his name to the month beginning at our Christmas, and who, as will be pointed out in Chapter XXIII, was closely related to the popular conception of Jesus. In the legend of the birth of the divine Ion, the mythical ancestor of the Ionians, again, the babe is placed in just such a basket in a cave.[2]

In the Gospel of St. Matthew, but nowhere else, we have the story that Joseph was warned in a dream of Herod's intention to kill the child, and that therefore he took Him to Egypt; and that in the meantime Herod caused all the infants of Bethlehem to be massacred.[3] Now, in the first place, Herod died in the year 4 B.C., and Jesus does not seem to have been born until the year 2 B.C. or 1 B.C. (a paradox due to the fact that the reckoning Anno Domini is a year or two out); and at any rate, Josephus, who fully records all the crimes of Herod, makes no mention of this massacre. Actu-

[1] Smith, *Dict. of Gr. and Rom. Antiq.*    [2] Euripides, *Ion.*
[3] Matt. ii. 13–21

52

ally, the story seems to be an echo of old Jewish legends, such as that of Nimrod, who is said to have tried to destroy the baby Abraham by slaughtering all the infants in his dominions;[1] that of the Pharaoh of Egypt who wished to kill all the Jewish firstborn;[2] and that of Joab who tried to kill the child Hadad by massacring the men of Edom,[3] Hadad escaping by flight into Egypt. There is also the story of the Roman Senate attempting by such a massacre to kill the baby Augustus.[4] At any rate its historicity is so very doubtful that the commemoration of the massacre in the Church calendar, and the reference to it in the Anglican collect for the day, might with profit be cancelled.

I may add that the time of year at which Jesus was born is completely unknown, the date of our Christmas Day, December 25th, having been adopted by the Church only in the Fourth Century A.D., this being the traditional date of the birth of the sun-god; but of this I will speak in a later

---

[1] E. Giran, *Jesus of Nazareth*, p. 49.     [2] Exodus i. 15.
[3] 1 Kings xi. 15.     [4] Suetonius, *Octavius*, 94.

chapter. Nothing, in fact, is known historically about the birth or early years of our Lord. All that can be said is that He was the son of a carpenter named Joseph and of his wife, probably called Mary,[1] who seem to have lived at Nazareth, or the neighbouring hamlet of Bethlehem. These two had at least seven children, there being five sons—Jesus, James, Joses, Judas, and Simon—and two or more daughters, whose names are not known;[2] and we may therefore picture our Lord as growing up with His brothers and sisters in the usual rough manner of a middle-class native household, but gradually detaching Himself from them as His religious consciousness developed.

Then, perhaps about the year A.D. 28 or 29, though the date is very uncertain, He set out upon His ministry; and from that time until His arrest in April, A.D. 30, the account of His wanderings is sufficiently full for us to be able to build up a clear picture of the Master. I will speak in the next chapter of the miracles and miraculous occurrences recorded in the Gospels,

[1] See Chapter IV.    [2] Mark vi. 3.

most of which can be discarded without loss to the story: it is only necessary here to point out that the historical personality of Jesus, and the supremacy of that personality, rest upon His sayings, backed up by the record of His behaviour as chronicled in the Synoptic Gospels. The sayings are to be regarded as, on the whole, authentic, for they are mostly derived from the two actual collections written down by Mark and Matthew, as Bishop Papias has recorded.[1]

Now, those critics[2] who hold that Jesus never lived, have been at pains to show that most of the things He said had been said before: for instance, "Blessed are the meek, for they shall inherit the earth,"[3] is the same as the Psalmist's "The meek shall inherit the land;"[4] "Whosoever shall smite thee on thy right cheek, turn to him the other also,"[5] is the same as Jeremiah's "He giveth his cheek to him that smiteth him,"[6] and

---

[1] See Chapter III.
[2] For instance, J. M. Robertson, *Christianity and Mythology*, p. 440 ff.
[3] Matt. v. 5.      [4] Psalm xxxvii. 11.      [5] Matt. v. 39.
[6] Lam. iii. 30.

Isaiah's "I give my cheeks to them that plucked out the hair";[1] and so forth. But one may go further than this, and may say that the wisdom of Jesus is the cream of the wisdom of all the philosophers, both Jewish and pagan; and yet that there is nothing in the Gospels to suggest that their authors could have been capable of searching the books of the world and of collecting this wisdom so as to make it seem to fall from the lips of one imaginary figure.

Nor can the authors of the Gospels, who delighted in wild tales of miracles and in all manner of incredible marvels, be deemed capable of having invented so sublime a figure as that of the simple, self-sacrificing, tender-hearted, gallant Jesus which their stories reveal. If ever there was an authentic personality in history, it is that of our Lord; and the removal of the miraculous element from the Gospels only serves to make Him stand out more clearly as the most perfect character the world has ever known.

The fact that so little is told us about His

[1] Isaiah lv. 6.

early years, and that in two of the Gospels the account begins only at His baptism by John, goes to prove that the writers of these books were not romancing. Had they been inventing the story they would have had a great deal to say about the manifestations of His divine nature during his youth.

# CHAPTER VI

## THE MIRACULOUS OCCURRENCES

THE earliest of the Gospels, that of St. Mark, did not assume its present form until between forty and seventy years after the death of our Lord, and the other Gospels are still later in date; and it is absolutely incredible that the stories about Him should have remained unexaggerated and unaugmented during that period. Tales about a popular hero invariably expand; and in the case of those relating to Jesus, who was accepted by His early followers at first as the God-sent Messiah and then as the Son of God incarnate on earth, it is impossible to believe that they would not gradually have been embellished, or that some of them would not have been developed around an insignificant nucleus, or unconsciously borrowed from other sources, or even invented. The marvel is not that there are so many, but that there are so few, improbable stories told about Him, since He was acknowledged to be divine, and therefore was presumed to have performed miracles and to have been the cause of miraculous occurrences. Far more incredible stories have been told about other people than about Jesus.

To take a single instance: just before Julius Cæsar was assassinated, all the doors and windows of his house are said to have burst open suddenly and of their own accord; strange lights were observed in the sky; weird noises were heard; phantoms glowing like red-hot metal were seen fighting; and so forth.[1] These, and hundreds of similar stories in connection with other persons, were the talk of the world at the time of the composition of the Gospels. Everybody believed in miraculous events, in signs and wonders; and it was always assumed that saintly or divine personages showed their power by performing miracles. Plotinus, the philosopher, is said to have performed them; Apollonius of Tyana is credited with many miracles; and those told of the early Christian saints

[1] Plutarch's Lives, *Cæsar.*

59

are far more numerous and far more extraordinary than are those of the Founder of the Faith.

But, as Rénan[1] so aptly puts it: "If ever the worship of Jesus loses its hold upon mankind, it will be precisely on account of those acts which originally inspired belief in Him." Times have changed, and we no longer need miraculous stories to support our acceptance of our Lord's divine mission. His historic life and His teachings form the basis of our convictions in regard to Him; and the tales of miracles or miraculous events which are to be considered as contrary to nature tend now towards disbelief rather than towards belief in Him.

Let us first consider the miraculous events. The story of the Virgin Birth, as I have pointed out in Chapter IV, is derived from pagan sources, and first appears in the Gospel of St. Luke, which dates from about a hundred years after the recorded event. The earliest Gospel, that of St. Mark, makes no reference to the birth at all; nor does the Gospel of St. John, which may have been

[1] E. Rénan, *Life of Jesus.*

written as early as A.D. 100; both chroniclers begin with our Lord's baptism by John, and it is therefore practically certain that nothing was known to their authors about His birth and youth. The Gospel of St. Luke, written about A.D. 100, alone tells the story of the angels appearing to the shepherds; but the Gospel of St. Matthew, dating from some ten years later, does not know anything about this legend, and gives in its place the tale of the star in the east and the wise men, which story was unknown to the others.

The story of the forty days in the wilderness and of the temptation by Satan is very briefly recorded in St. Mark, the earliest Gospel.[1] We are told no more than that Jesus was in the wilderness for this length of time, that He was tempted by the Devil, and that the angels ministered to Him: the whole story is dismissed in one verse, and there is no mention of His fasting. The Gospel of St. John does not relate the story at all. Only St. Luke (A.D. 100) and St. Matthew (A.D. 110) give the account of how Jesus fasted,

[1] Mark i. 13.

how Satan took Him on to a mountain and on to a pinnacle of the Temple, how he tempted Him, and how the Evil One was defeated in argument.

The retirement to the wilderness may well be an historical fact, but the story of the temptation is an obvious allegory to be understood in a spiritual sense, though the source of some of the details may be traced. The hoofed god Pan is the prototype of Satan, and there is a pagan legend which relates how the young Jupiter was led by Pan to the top of a mountain, from which he could see the countries of the world.[1] This mountain was called the "Pillar of Heaven," which perhaps explains the introduction of the pinnacle of the temple into the story. Zoroaster, the founder of the Persian religion, went into the wilderness, and was tempted by the Devil; Buddha did likewise, and was tempted; Moses and Elijah had both dwelt in the wilderness, and the former fasted on Sinai forty days, while the latter fasted on Horeb forty days; Ezekiel had to bear the iniquity of the house of Judah for forty days; the destruction

[1] Lactantius, *Divine Institutes*, i. 11.

# THE MIRACULOUS OCCURRENCES

of mankind in the Deluge lasted forty days; there were forty nights of mourning in the mysteries of the pagan Proserpine; there were forty days of sacrifice in the old Persian "Salutation of Mithra"; and so forth.

In regard to the miraculous events which took place at the death of Jesus, the Gospel of St. John says nothing, and those of St. Mark and St. Luke speak only of the rending of the veil of the temple and of the darkness or overcasting of the sky for three hours. The story of the earthquake, the upheaval of the rocks, the bursting open of the graves, and the appearance of the dead, is alone related in St. Matthew's Gospel, written nearly eighty years after the event, and is therefore not certainly authentic. Of course there is no reason why an earthquake should not have occurred on that day, but if it had really taken place it is almost inconceivable that none of the three earlier Gospels should have mentioned it.

Now as to the miracles performed by Jesus. The turning of the water into wine at Cana may be based on similar tales told in regard to Dionysos,

63

who was one of the most popular gods of early
Christian times; for the Church has fixed January
6th as the anniversary of the miracle, and that
date corresponds to the festival of Dionysos at
which the changing of water into wine was believed
to take place as an annual miracle at certain
centres of his worship.[1]   The feeding of the multi-
tude with five loaves and two fishes is practically
the same as the miracle performed by Elisha,[2]
and the story may therefore be regarded as having
been copied from the earlier legend.   The calming
of the tempest may be a story which developed
from an actual incident wherein a providential
calm presently happened to follow an ejaculation
uttered by Jesus.   The story of the walking on
the sea, as simply related in the earliest Gospel,
may have developed from a misunderstanding, the
Greek permitting of the translation "walking *beside*
the sea," instead of "*on* the sea."   St. Luke's Gospel
does not mention the incident; and the more
elaborate version of the story, in which Peter tries
also to walk on the water and falls in, is, as usual,

[1] Athenæus, i. 61.                    [2] 2 Kings iv. 42.

only to be found in the latest Gospel compiled after the best part of a century had elapsed.

The raising from the dead of the son of the widow of Nain is only mentioned in St. Luke, and the raising of Lazarus only in St. John; and it may safely be said that if these two astounding miracles had really occurred, every Gospel would have recorded them, for they would have been the most mighty ever performed by Jesus. The raising of the daughter of Jairus, on the other hand, is not a miracle: Jesus denied that the girl was dead, but rightly said that she was in a cataleptic state; and His words to her were not the gentle: "Damsel, I say unto thee arise!" but a sharp order, "*Talitha! Cumi!*"—"Girl! Get up!"[1]

The miracles of healing, and of casting out devils which we should now term the successful treatment of the epileptic, the neurasthenic or the insane, are such as have been performed time and again by the power of mind over matter: they are perfectly credible, and are not now regarded by science as outside natural laws. Jesus did not

[1] Mark v. 41.

consider His healings as miracles, but as ordinary faith-cures; and He was wont to say: "*Thy faith hath made thee whole.*"[1] He often showed great reluctance to use His undoubtedly extraordinary powers. "Why doth this generation seek after a sign?" He asked. "There shall no sign be given unto this generation." He opposed the idea that His Messianic claims should be supported in this way; and He said that what He did was no more than what could be done by any man of high spiritual attainment.[2] In His own home, as is so frankly recorded, there was not enough faith in Him for Him to effect any noteworthy cures.[3]

Therefore, in considering the miracles and miraculous occurrences, we are justified in believing only those which can be considered credible; and in regard to both we are entitled to allow for the growth of the stories during the period between the lifetime of our Lord and the compiling of the Gospels. This growth is of the very nature of things, and cannot be overlooked; and when, be-

[1] Matt. ix. 22.　　　[2] Mark xi. 23.　　　[3] Mark vi. 5.

sides this, we remember that any impossible tale of this kind could have been told of Jesus at that time with the presumption that, since He was the Son of God, it would be believed, the fact that the really incredible stories are so few in number speaks highly for the restraint of the authors of the Gospels.

The modern thinker has carefully to guard against the fallacious idea that the time of Christ was so long ago that things then happened which do not happen now. Actually, life was lived in those days under precisely the same natural conditions as it is at present; and, indeed, nineteen centuries is not a great length of time. It is easily covered by fifty generations: that is to say, all our ancestors back to the days of our Lord could be comfortably carried on one ordinary London omnibus. Or, if we reckon in units of the proverbial span of life, we may say that Jesus lived no more than twenty-seven lifetimes ago. Thus, anything which is said to have happened then must be tested by the same rules of probability as would be applied in the case of stories of modern events.

# CHAPTER VII

## THE CRUCIFIXION AND THE BARABBAS SACRIFICE

THE study of ancient religious customs provides no stranger or more complex puzzle than that of the relationship between the Gospel story of the Crucifixion of our Lord and the ancient rituals of human sacrifice. At first sight the account of the Crucifixion seems to be quite straightforward, and to describe an ordinary Roman infliction of death upon the cross: that is to say, Jesus seems to have been put to death by the usual method employed by the Romans in the case of criminals of low class; but when we look closer we find that some of the main incidents in the Gospel account have their parallels in these rites of human sacrifice as practised by the ancients. In fact, one may say that if a cosmopolitan writer of that period had set himself to *invent* the story of the sacrificial death of an incarnate god who was

68

thought to have died for the remission of sins, he might, out of his general knowledge, have produced a tale more or less like that in the Gospels.

. This startling fact has led a good many critics to regard the whole story of the Crucifixion as a myth, while others take the view that although the account of the execution of Jesus is correct in so far as the main fact is concerned—namely, that He suffered the Roman death penalty of crucifixion—the details are fictitious additions derived from a knowledge of the usual rites and procedure of human sacrifice as it was still practised at that time in some parts of the Roman Empire. In other words, according to these critics, the authors of the Gospels had wished to show that the earthly task of Jesus had culminated in the sacrifice of Himself to God, and therefore they had framed a story which was not that of an ordinary crucifixion of a criminal, but was that of an actual human sacrifice.

It is, indeed, impossible to avoid the conclusion that this was no ordinary Roman crucifixion of which the Gospels tell us: there were some peculiar features about it which distinguished it from the usual execution upon the cross. Five of these peculiarities may here be mentioned. Firstly, this death by crucifixion was inflicted upon a man whose crime was that of blasphemy and heresy, but the punishment for such a crime was death by decapitation or stoning. Secondly, the execution took place on the eve of the Passover; and since crucifixion was a slow torture, often lasting several days before death released the sufferer, an ordinary crucifixion would have been held over until after the festival. Thirdly, in spite of it being the day before the Passover, two malefactors were also crucified. Fourthly, the victim in this case was first dressed up as a King, a mock crown being placed on His head, and a mock sceptre in His hand; and in the inscription affixed to the cross He was described as "the King of the Jews." And, finally, the execution of Jesus was preceded by the release of a condemned criminal called Barabbas.

It is the last of these points which, in my opinion, furnishes the clue to the mystery. I believe that the Crucifixion of Jesus *was* regarded by the Jews as a sort of human sacrifice, and that therefore the similarity of the procedure described in the Gospels to the old sacrificial ritual, far from providing evidence that the story was invented, indicates that the account is authentic history. But to prove my argument it must be shown firstly that the Jews of those days did practise some kind of human sacrifice by crucifixion annually on the eve of the Passover and, secondly, that Jesus was their chosen victim for that year's sacrificial ceremony. The matter is of immense importance, for if I am right the main argument advanced by that powerful school of criticism which regards Jesus as a mythical figure completely collapses, or rather, is turned round to demonstrate His historicity.

In primitive days it was the custom in many lands for a king or ruler to put his own son to death as a sacrifice to the tribal god. Philo of Byblus[1] in his book on the Jews says that it was customary for the king to give his beloved son

[1] Quoted by Eusebius, *Preparatio Evang.*, i. 10, 29.

to die for the nation as a ransom offered to the avenging devils, and that the victims were sacrificed with mystic rites. Porphyry tells us[1] that Phœnician history is full of such sacrifices, and we know that amongst the Canaanites not only kings but ordinary people sacrificed their children. Amongst the numerous instances of this custom on record, I may mention the following well-known cases. There is the shocking story[2] of how Abraham, impelled by religious motives, attempted to sacrifice his son Isaac; and there is the even more appalling tale of King David's effort to stop a famine by sacrificing seven princes of the royal house, the sons of King Saul, and hanging them up before the Lord.[3] The Bible also tells how King Mesha of Moab sacrificed his eldest son;[4] how King Hiel sacrificed his sons at the foundation of Jericho;[5] and how Kings Ahaz and Manasseh consigned their children to the sacrificial fire;[6] and there is an Arab legend that Ishmael, like

---

[1] Porphyry, *De Abstinentia*, ii. 56.   [2] Genesis xxii. 1–19.
[3] 2 Sam. xxi. 9.   [4] 2 Kings iii. 27.
[5] 1 Kings xvi. 34.   [6] 2 Chron. xxviii. 3; xxxiii. 6.

Isaac, was nearly sacrificed by his father.[1] The Carthaginians, who originally came from Syria, also had this custom: Hamilcar sacrificed his son at the siege of Agrigentum;[2] and Maleus, a Carthaginian general, crucified his son as a sacrifice to Baal.[3] The words of the prophet Micah may also be noted: "Shall I give my firstborn for my transgression, the fruit of my body for the sin of my soul?"[4]

The king was, in early times, usually regarded as a personification of the tribal god, and hence as the divine father of his people, and his son who was sacrificed was thus the "Son of the Father," this phrase being in Hebrew *Bar Abbas*. But, as civilised ideas developed, kings were gradually relieved of this terrible duty, and in various lands a criminal condemned to death was substituted for the royal prince. Thus in the Babylonian Sacæa a criminal was dressed up in royal robes to represent a prince, a crown being placed on his head, and was scourged and then crucified or

[1] Weil, *Biblical Legends of the Mussulmans*, p. 62.
[2] Diodorus, xiii. 86.    [3] Justin, xviii. 7.    [4] Micah vi. 7.

hanged;[1] and similarly at Rhodes a criminal was sacrificed at the Kronian festival[2] in commemoration, obviously, of the sacrifice by Kronos of his royal son Ieoud. It may well be, therefore, that in early Palestine a similar custom obtained, and that a criminal was sacrificed in the guise of the primitive royal "Son of the Father," or *Bar Abbas*.

Now the sacrifice of a lamb or kid at the great Jewish festival of the Passover undoubtedly had its origin in a human sacrifice, the Passover being really a spring festival very much older than the days of the Exodus; for in the story of Abraham and Isaac, it will be remembered, Isaac is described as playing the part of the sacrificial lamb, and finally a ram is substituted for him: a tradition which may have actually been cited by way of authority for the substitution of the animal for the human victim, this substitution of a lamb for the first-born son being definitely affirmed in the Mosaic law.[3] The above-mentioned sacrifice of Saul's sons, too, may have been connected with the prim-

[1] J. M. Robertson, *Pagan Christs*, p. 145.
[2] Porphyry, *De Abstinentia*, ii. 54.     [3] Exodus xxxiv. 20.

itive Passover, for the Bible says that they were sacrificed at the beginning of the barley harvest, and this harvest begins, in the plain of Jericho and in the Jordan Valley, at about the time of the Passover. There is a record, too, of a certain Jesus ben Pandira who was stoned to death and hung up on a tree on the eve of the Passover in the reign of Alexander Jannæus about 100 B.C.[1]

Thus, there is good reason to suppose that while the primitive human sacrifice at this great spring festival was transformed into the sacrifice of a lamb, the older custom also survived in a modified form, the execution of a condemned criminal being made to serve as a sort of human sacrifice performed annually at the time of the Passover; and since in primitive times the most efficacious sacrifice was that of a royal prince by his father the king, this criminal was made to play the part of a royal personage, as in the Babylonian Sacæa, being designated the *Bar Abbas* of the year. This would account for the remark attributed to Caiaphas,[2] that it was expedient, presumably at

[1] See Chapter II.                    [2] John xi. 50.

Passover-time,[1] that a man should be sacrificed
for the good of the nation; and it would also
explain the curious Gospel story of Barabbas.

Frazer has pointed out[2] that "Barrabas" was
certainly not the personal name of any one criminal, but was the traditional name for the victim
in an annual human sacrifice, or rather in the
execution into which the sacrifice had deteriorated;
and there is evidence that the use of this name
survived even later than the time of Christ, for
Philo Judæus,[3] writing in the days of Agrippa,
about A.D. 40, tells us that the mob at Alexandria
dressed up a crazy old man, putting a sham crown
on his head, a sceptre in his hand, and a purple
robe over his body, and hailing him as *Karabbas*,
an obvious miswriting for *Barabbas*, and as *Maris*,
the Syrian word for a royal personage.

In the Gospel story Pilate seems to have been
asked by the Jews to release to them the condemned criminal chosen to be the Barabbas for
that year—in this case the leader in some for-

[1] John xi. 55.   [2] Frazer, *Golden Bough.*
[3] Philo Judæus, *Against Flaccus*, ch. 6.

gotten riot; and, though the significance of the incident does not seem to have been understood at the time when it was recorded, the inference is that Jesus was made to take this man's place as that year's Barabbas. Now in these "Barabbas" executions the victim was always, it seems, crowned and dressed up as a royal personage, as in the above-mentioned case quoted by Philo Judæus. In the Kronos legend Ieoud was dressed in royal robes before being sacrificed; in the Babylonian Sacæa the victim was similarly robed and crowned; and the Carthaginian Maleus likewise dressed up his son as a royal personage before crucifying him. The significance of the dressing up of our Lord as a king, and of the inscription "The King of the Jews," thus becomes apparent.

The victims of these human sacrifices were generally crucified, or else killed and then "hung on a tree" until the evening, as in the various hangings before the Lord mentioned in the Bible.[1] In this regard it is interesting to notice that in the

[1] 2 Sam. xxi. 9; Josh. viii. 29; Josh. x. 26; etc.

Acts[1] the writer mistakenly speaks of Jesus as having been slain and then hanged on a tree, as though this were a common phrase coming readily to his mind; and the word "hanged" is frequently used in Greek to denote crucifixion.[2] In the holy groves of Upsala men were sacrificed by being hung up on the sacred trees;[3] the ancient Gauls crucified the human beings sacrificed to their gods;[4] the victim in the Babylonian Sacæa was crucified; the Carthaginian Maleus sacrificed his son by crucifixion; Jesus ben Pandira was hung up on a tree; and so forth. Although only one man represented the actual *Bar Abbas*, it must have been usual to sacrifice others with him; for it was customary in primitive days for persons to be slain on the occasion of an important death, so that their spirits should attend their prince into the next world.[5] Thus two men were crucified with Jesus, and the Gospels say explicitly that the

[1] Acts v. 30; x. 39.
[2] Frazer, *Golden Bough*, i. 226, note.
[3] Adam of Bremen, *Descriptio insularum Aquilonis*, 27.
[4] Strabo, bk. iv., ch. iv. 5.
[5] See, for example, Herodotus, iv. 71.

one was placed on His right hand and the other on His left, as though they were attendants. Moreover, in a fragment of Ctesias, it is recorded that the Egyptian usurper Inarus was crucified by Artaxerxes I between two thieves; and a Persian saint, Hitzibouzit, of unknown date, is said to have been "offered up as a sacrifice between two malefactors on a hill-top facing the sun."[1]

To sum up, then, if this theory be accepted, the fact that our Lord was put to death by crucifixion, and not, as in the case of John the Baptist, by decapitation, is explained; the reason why He was executed on the eve of the Passover becomes apparent; the purpose of dressing Him up in royal robes is shown; the significance of the release of "Barrabas" is made clear; and the presence of the two malefactors is accounted for. In this way the critical argument that the Gospel story of the Crucifixion is too similar to an account of a human sacrifice to be believed is disposed of. It *was* a human sacrifice.

[1] Conybeare, *Apology and Acts of Apollonius*, p. 270.

# CHAPTER VIII

### OTHER FEATURES OF THE CRUCIFIXION

IN the previous chapter I attempted to show that the Gospel story of the Crucifixion relates certain details which can best be accounted for on the supposition that Jesus was crucified in the guise of the annual *Bar Abbas*. But since this *Bar Abbas* victim appears to have been at that time always a condemned criminal, the disgrace of the execution was not mitigated, nor was the sacrificial character of His death at first any comfort to the disciples. The crucifixion of evil-doers, preceded by scourging, was, at the time of Christ, the usual Roman form of execution in the case of slaves or particularly rascally criminals; and its ignominy must have been bitterly felt, in spite of the fact that the Jews had given it this sacrificial aspect. But gradually the believers began to attribute a symbolical meaning to these events; and though this interpretation belongs to a period of a few years later, and was influenced by Gentile as well as Jewish thought, mention may here be made of some of the features of the execution which opened the way for religious speculation.

In the first place there was the fact that Jesus had been put to death by being exposed upon a cross, or, as the phrase was, hung upon a tree; for long before the Christian era a cross was widely used as an object of worship. Just as in Egypt the obelisk was not only a symbol of the sun-god, but was also itself a god, so the cross was itself an actual divinity. The trunk of a tree, with or without its branches, was sacred to various gods, and, in the case of the worship of Attis, the image of the god was hung upon his sacred pine-tree at the commemoration of his death; and we learn that the tree-trunk itself was swathed in linen and treated as an object of worship.[1] So, too, the tree sacred to Osiris was decked in linen and placed in the temple,[2] his body having traditionally been affixed in its branches.

[1] Frazer, *Adonis Attis Osiris*, p. 166.
[2] Firmicus Maternus, *De errore profanarum religionum*, xxvii. 1.

# PAGANISM IN OUR CHRISTIANITY

A clear instance of the worship of the cross, or tree, as itself a god is to be found in the half-pagan, half-Christian poem inscribed upon the early Anglo-Saxon cross at Ruthwell in Dumfriesshire.[1] In this poem the cross is made to say: "I lifted up Heaven's great lord, and they reviled us both together; me, stained with the blood poured from the man's side, and Christ who was on the cross. Then came nobles to Him in grief; and I, who beheld all, I was stricken with sorrow." Indeed, on the early church crucifixes Jesus is represented not as a nude and dying or dead man, but as a glorified divinity, alive and clothed in a robe: which suggests that, through the persistence of the pagan tradition, He was in some sense identified with the older divinity of the cross or tree itself.

In the previous chapter it has been shown that crucifixion was practised in several lands in the sacred ceremony of human sacrifice, as though it had a special religious significance; and to the instances there cited I may add that of Cyrus, who

[1] Weigall, *Wanderings in Anglo-Saxon Britain*, p. 140

at one time was thought by the Jews to be the Messiah, and who, according to one account, was crucified.[1] Prometheus, too, whose legendary history provides the most famous instance of a pagan god who suffered for mankind, is said by Lucan to have been crucified.[2] In fact, so widespread was the understanding of crucifixion as meaning the pious bearing of suffering, not as a punishment but as a sacrifice, that the word was used, long before the time of Christ, in regard to all kinds of sorrows and afflictions wherein there was no suggestion of dishonour. Thus, when St. Paul spoke of "the preaching of the cross" he meant the preaching of the doctrine of religious suffering and pain such as the sacrificial victim endured; and he must have used the expression in the knowledge that it would be perfectly intelligible to pagan minds, crucifixion being a theological commonplace. And when he wrote: "O, foolish Galatians, who hath bewitched you that ye should not obey the truth, before whose eyes Jesus Christ hath

[1] Diodorus Siculus, ii. 44.
[2] J. M. Robertson, *Pagan Christs*, p. 167, note 5.

been evidently set forth crucified among you?"[1] he meant "Why do you not grasp the truth, when you see that Jesus Christ endured that traditional rite of sacrificial sufferings by crucifixion which you know all religion demands?"

Next, we come to the matter of the breaking of the legs of the two malefactors, and the proposal to break those of Jesus, which was abandoned because He was already dead. The breaking of the legs in ordinary criminal crucifixion was a means of shortening the victim's life. Crucifixion was the fastening of a man to a cross or tree in order that he might die of exposure and strain, generally after many days. His hands were tied, and sometimes nailed also, to the cross-beam or branches, and his feet rested upon a projection from the upright post or trunk; and, so long as the legs were strong enough to support the body, no direct cause of death was present. But if the legs were broken, all the weight of the body would depend from the arms, and the heart's action would soon be stopped, death thus being caused without "blood-guiltiness"

[1] Gal. iii. 1.

on the part of any one man such as would be the case if a mortal blow were inflicted.

Now the fact that Jesus had suffered on the eve of the Passover, taken together with the fact that having died so quickly on the cross He had escaped having His legs broken, must have given rise to an excited train of speculation; for the coincidence identified Him with the Paschal lamb, traditionally killed on the eve of the Passover for the remission of sins, the bones of which were not allowed to be broken. I have already pointed out that in the primitive Passover a human victim was probably sacrificed, a lamb being later substituted; and it was a widespread custom in human sacrifice to break the limbs of the victim in order that he should not struggle, but should appear to die voluntarily, it being regarded as essential that "sacrificial victims should be of a willing mind."[1] When an unalarmed dumb animal was substituted for the terrified human being, however, there was not often any struggling to be prevented; and

[1] Tertullian, *Ad Scapulam*, 2. See also Macrobius, *Sat.*, iii. 5; and Lucan, *Pharsalia*, i. 611.

therefore the law was able to decree that the limbs should not be broken. Jesus thus seemed to be the voluntary Paschal sacrifice *par excellence*, offered up for the redemption of man, without resistance and without the breaking of the bones; and everything mystically denoted by that voluntary sacrifice was applied to Him.

Then, again, there was the fact that the side of Jesus had been pierced by a lance. Actually what had happened was that a soldier had pricked His side to ascertain that He was dead, just as Panteus pricked the bodies of Cleomenes and his companions to see if life were extinct.[1] It must be remembered that it was very remarkable that Jesus had died so soon: the victims of crucifixion generally lingered for days, and there is a case on record of a certain Mansûr al-Hallaj, a Sufi of the Ninth Century A.D., who was nailed to a cross for four days, and then, having been pardoned, was taken down not much the worse for his experience. The soldier very naturally, therefore, pricked Jesus with his lance to assure himself that He was not alive.

[1] Plutarch's Lives, *Cleomenes*.

## OTHER FEATURES OF THE CRUCIFIXION

But the Gentile followers of our Lord must have seen in this incident a further indication that He was indeed a mystical sacrifice; for the infliction of such a wound on a sacrificial victim was a widespread custom. Strabo tells us[1] that the primitive Albanians used to sacrifice a human being to the moon-goddess by piercing his side with a sacred spear; and in the spring sacrifice at Salamis the human victim was similarly pierced by a lance.[2] So, also, in the human sacrifices to Odin the victims were strung up on the sacred tree, and, when dead, were pierced by a spear;[3] and in the worship of Mithra, the bull, which was identical with Mithra himself, was stabbed in the side, as can be seen in the well-known Mithraic sculptures.[4]

In order that the reader may clearly understand the argument of those who believe that Jesus never lived, let me summarise these features of the Crucifixion story (discussed in this and the previ-

[1] Strabo, xi. 4, sec. 7.
[2] Eusebius, *Præp. Evang.*, iv. 16.
[3] Frazer, *Adonis Attis Osiris*, p. 186, note 6.
[4] British Museum and elsewhere.

ous chapter) which connect it with human sacrifice and which therefore have seemed to critics to indicate that the whole account was an invention drawn from the writers' knowledge of sacrificial procedure. These features are (1) the death by crucifixion, (2) on the eve of the Passover, (3) with two other victims, one on either side, (4) after the dressing up in royal robes, and (5) after the release of a prisoner called Barabbas; and also (6) the proposal to break the victims' legs, and (7) the piercing of the side with a lance. All these features are so well known in the rites of human sacrifice that the attitude of these critics is not surprising. But my contention is that the first five were features of the *Bar Abbas* sacrifice, and that Jesus *was* the *Bar Abbas* victim; and that the other two were ordinary occurrences which, by a coincidence, corresponded to sacrificial usages.

At any rate there can be no doubt that the early Christians, even before the time of St. Paul,[1] came to think of the Crucifixion as sacrificial, and, in fact, that the preaching of "Christ Crucified" was

[1] 1 Cor. xv. 3.

one of the main features of the new faith. Judaism
and paganism had alike implanted in men's minds
a sense of awe of the cross as an ancient divine
thing, and had familiarised them with the idea of
a divinity sacrificially crucified; and gradually the
crucified Jesus took the place of the preaching
Jesus as the centre of the religion.

To-day, however, the thinking layman is con-
centrating less on the sacramentally slain God-
incarnate, and is turning more and more to the
man Jesus, the teacher of divine truths, the supreme example of the perfect life which braved
death itself for the sake of mankind's uplifting;
and His crucifixion, which theology regards as the
sacramental purpose and point of His incarnation,
is beginning to be defined simply as the inevitable
result of His gallant opposition to conventional
religion, and the crowning instance of His heroism.
Those who look thus to the Master's life as an
example to be followed, rather than to His death
as a mystic propitiation for sin, are tending to see
something of a mental retrogression in the increasing sanctity attributed to the symbol of the cross

in the Church. Crucifix-worship, like its concomitant tree-worship, is, in fact, too closely
related to paganism to be up to the intellectual
standard demanded by a modern religion.

# CHAPTER IX

## THE RESURRECTION

ANY student who understands the mentality of the men of the First Century will realise that the original Christians believed Jesus to be the incarnate Son of God largely because they were convinced that, after being sacrificially crucified, His dead body had come to life again. While He was with them His disciples had regarded Him as Son of God in the sense that He was the God-sent Messiah or Christ; but when He appeared to them in the flesh after they had seen Him die on the cross they were stirred into an enthusiastic certainty that, though distinct from God, He was divine, since in so many contemporary religions the incarnate god was supposed to die and to come back to life again amidst general rejoicings.

To-day, nearly two thousand years later, the point of view has changed. We regard Jesus Christ as divine because of the perfection of His life and teachings; and while the belief that His spiritual self returned to God is essential to the creed, the question as to whether His body—as distinct from that spiritual entity—really did come back to life after being dead is a matter not of tremendous consequence. Nobody in his senses now believes that Jesus ascended into Heaven in "His body, with flesh, bones, and all things appertaining to the perfection of man's nature," as the obsolete 4th Article of Religion in the Anglican Prayer Book says. Modern Christians believe in a spiritual ascension, but not in an ascension of the body; and therefore the bodily resurrection of our Lord becomes relatively unimportant, because at His spiritual ascension His body must anyhow have died or been cast aside.

The orthodox Christian belief to-day is that Jesus suffered temporary death upon the cross on the Friday and was placed in the tomb on the same evening; that before dawn on the Sunday He came back to life and left the tomb; that during the next forty days or so[1] He was seen alive and in

[1] Acts i. 3.

the flesh; and that He then ascended spiritually into heaven, His mortal body disintegrating or being discarded.

The Jews think that His body was stolen from the tomb, and that the stories of His subsequent appearances are fictitious; and Tertullian[1] (born about A.D. 160) records the story that the body was removed by the man in charge of the garden wherein the sepulchre was situated, so that the visitors to the tomb should not spoil his lettuces. The Mohammedans believe that a man resembling Him was crucified as a substitute, and that Jesus survived, this doctrine being recorded in the Koran,[2] and being derived apparently from the Basilidans, who used to say definitely that Simon of Cyrene was the man substituted. But there is the ring of truth in most of the details of the story as told in the Gospels, and an impartial critic can hardly fail to believe Jesus did appear, alive and in the flesh, after the Crucifixion. Let us run through the account of these events as we have it in the New Testament.

[1] Tertullian, *De Spectaculis*.     [2] *Sura* iv.

Pilate did not wish to condemn Jesus, and the centurion in charge of the arrangements was also in sympathy with Him. After Jesus had been on the cross only a short time He was given something to drink, and almost immediately expired. Joseph of Arimathæa, a secret disciple, at once went to Pilate and asked to be allowed to take Him down from the cross: but Pilate was amazed to hear that He was so soon dead, for, as has already been pointed out, the victims of crucifixion usually lingered for several days. He therefore questioned the centurion, who replied that Jesus was indeed dead, whereupon he authorised Joseph to take the body down.

Joseph, helped, according to one Gospel, by Nicodemus, another secret disciple, then wrapped Jesus in some linen and laid Him temporarily in a new tomb cut out of the rock within a private garden; and he and his men rolled a big boulder against the door. The women who had been in the following of our Lord, having seen where He was laid, went home and prepared the soap and scents usually employed in washing the dead, with a view to burying the body properly immediately after the Sabbath (Saturday). Meanwhile, so says St. Matthew's Gospel, which is the latest of the Synoptics, a guard of soldiers was placed on the tomb, for fear lest the disciples should steal the body; but this detail, omitted by the earlier accounts, may not be authentic.

Before daybreak on the Sunday morning the two Marys and some others came to the tomb to wash the body, and found the stone rolled away from the entrance. In the earliest Gospel, that of St. Mark, they then saw "a young man sitting on the right side, clothed in a long white garment"; in the Gospel of St. John this man has become two angelic figures in white; in that of St. Luke these two figures are said to have been wearing shining robes; and in the latest Synoptic Gospel, that of St. Matthew, written 70 or 80 years after the event, the two have developed into actual angels with faces like lightning and robes like snow. According to the St. Mark account these words were then addressed to the frightened women: "Do not be afraid. You are looking for

Jesus of Nazareth who was crucified, are you not? He is risen: he is not here. Look!—that is the place where they laid him. But go away now, and tell his followers and Peter that he is going on ahead into Galilee, and there you will find him, as he told you."[1]

St. Mark says that the women then ran away, and did not dare to tell anybody of what they had seen, but that later in the day Mary Magdalene actually saw Jesus, though when she told the disciples they would not believe her. St. Luke's Gospel also says that the women told the incredulous disciples, but that Peter then went to the tomb, and saw the linen clothes lying there. St. Matthew's Gospel says that the women saw Jesus near the tomb, and that He said to them: "Do not be afraid. Go and tell my brethren to go into Galilee, and there they will find me."[2]

St. John's Gospel gives a different account. Mary Magdalene was the first at the tomb, and she ran and told Peter and John that the body of Jesus had been removed, but that she did not

[1] Mark xvi. 6, 7.   [2] Matt. xxviii. 10.

know where it had been taken to; whereupon these two men went to the tomb, and Peter saw the linen clothes lying there, and the napkin, which had covered the face, folded up and lying separately. Returning, Mary then saw the two angelic figures, after which, turning round, she saw a man whom she thought to be the gardener, and said to him, "If you have taken him away, tell me where you have put him." The supposed gardener, however, proved to be Jesus Himself, evidently dressed in labourer's clothes.

Now these stories have been pronounced by many critics to be entirely fiction; but to me they seem to be palpably authentic. They show, however, that Jesus had not passed beyond recall upon the cross, but that, having sunk into a condition indistinguishable from death, He was carried to the sepulchre, where He recovered, and was perhaps given somebody's clothes to wear, which led to His being mistaken for the gardener. In this case the supposed angelic figures seen by the two Marys would have been mortal men who had helped our Lord during the night. In support of

this theory it is to be observed that He had not
been much hurt by being crucified. It was not
the custom to drive nails through the feet, for
the victim usually stood upon a block projecting
from the cross; and the Gospel of St. John speaks
of His hands being wounded but not His feet.
The victim's arms were generally tied to the cross-
beam, and if the hands were nailed it was only as
an added insult, a small nail being driven through
the flesh of each hand, between the fingers, without causing a serious wound. A soldier had
pricked our Lord's side to see if He were dead,
but this wound, also, might have been slight; and
in other respects He would have been little the
worse for the short exposure on the cross.

This theory is not so heretical as it seems, and
though the ordinary Christian will protest that
our Lord's resurrection from the dead is the very
foundation of the faith, careful thought will show
that actually no faith would be worth consideration
which based itself merely on the apparent coming
to life of a dead body. To the modern religious
mind, in fact, there can be very little difference

in saying, as do the orthodox, that Jesus was temporarily dead, but after a few hours came to life again, and saying, as do the critics, that He passed into a condition indistinguishable from death, and then returned to life. It leaves the idea of His heroic and supreme sacrifice unaffected, for He certainly expected death; nor does it affect the more mystical interpretation of the Passion, for even modern science cannot define the difference between death and a death-like condition before mortification sets in.

The Gospel stories then proceed to tell us how He appeared to the disciples, and they are emphatic that He was alive and was not merely a spirit. St. Mark's Gospel says that He was seen by two men who were walking into the country, and then by the eleven as they sat at dinner. St. John's Gospel tells how He appeared to the eleven, and did so again after eight days. St. Luke tells the story of His walking with the two men on the way to Emmaus, and of His coming in to the disciples at dinner. This account reveals the fact that He tried hard to convince them that

He was alive, saying: "Handle me, and see; for a spirit would not have flesh and bones as you see I have."[1] He then asked them, as well a hungry outlaw might, whether they had anything for Him to eat; and they gave Him some fish and some honey, after eating which He led them as far as Bethany, two miles from Jerusalem, and then departed.

St. Matthew's Gospel says that He made a rendezvous in the hills of Galilee, and there met them; and in the Acts we are told that He preached to them and remained in touch with them for some forty days; while St. Paul says that five hundred persons saw Him at one time.[2] But the last appearance to be described in detail is that which is recorded in the Gospel of St. John, when, early one morning, the disciples who were fishing in the lake of Tiberias (the Sea of Galilee) saw Him on the shore, and He asked them for food. Obviously, this was no spirit: it was a man in hiding; and the last picture we have of Him shows Him cooking some fish over a fire out here in the open in the grey light of dawn.

[1] Luke xxiv. 39.　　　　　　　　　[2] 1 Cor. xv. 6.

# THE RESURRECTION

Such is the circumstantial story as given in the Gospels for the purpose of proving that He was alive. This it does prove, in my opinion; but what happened after that is a deep mystery. The orthodox Christian is entitled to say that the divine, spiritual part of Him immediately ascended to God; but whether this occurred at once or not, in the end His mortal body must have died and returned to dust. It is to His spiritual resurrection and ascension that we now look, in the faith that on earth and in heaven His divine Being is eternal.

# CHAPTER X

## THE ASCENSION AND THE MESSIAHSHIP

THE earliest Christians had a story of their Master to tell which, when cleared of the colouring and embellishments put upon it in the fervour of their excitement and love, was somewhat as follows. The adored and revered Jesus had gone about the country preaching and healing the sick in a most godlike manner, and in the end had admitted that He was the promised Messiah. He had been acclaimed by his followers as the national Saviour, but, to their bitter disappointment, His entry into Jerusalem had failed to impress the bulk of the populace; and He had been arrested and crucified on the eve of the Passover, thereby changing their hopes into despair and perplexity. They had seen Him die upon the cross on that Friday afternoon; but on the third day, the Sunday morning, the tomb in which He had been laid was found open, and soon afterwards He had appeared before them, alive. Thereafter He had been seen by them on several occasions, and had talked to them, explaining how the old prophecies required that the Messiah should be rejected and executed; and, their eyes having thus been opened, their sorrow had been turned into joy, and they had realised that He was indeed the Christ. Later, apparently in Galilee, hundreds of people had seen Him; but at last He had left them, and though two messengers from Him had come to them, telling them that He would return,[1] He never came back.

Such was the historic and basic story upon which the faith was founded; and there are two points in it which must now be considered—the Ascension and the fulfilment of the Messianic prophecies. The Ascension is not mentioned in the earliest Christian writings, namely, the Epistles; nor, apparently, was it referred to in the earliest Gospel, that of St. Mark, for the words,

[1] Acts i. 10, gives the version of this incident current 50 to 70 years later.

"He was received up into heaven,"[1] are quite vague and are included in those last twelve verses of the book which are now recognised by practically all Biblical scholars as a much later addition.[2] The Gospels of St. Matthew and St. John do not mention the Ascension. It is only recorded in the writings attributed to St. Luke, namely, the Gospel of that name and the Acts, both of which date probably from round about A.D. 100: in the Gospel it is related that Jesus blessed His disciples and "was parted from them," it being added, perhaps as a presumption, that He was taken up into heaven;[3] but in the Acts it is definitely said that He was taken up in the presence of His followers, ascending until a cloud hid Him, and left them staring at the sky.[4]

Now the fact that there is, thus, only one clear record of the Ascension, this being in a work written some fifty to seventy years after the sup-

---

[1] Mark xvi. 19.

[2] Even so orthodox a writer as Bishop Goodwin (*Foundations of the Creed*, p. 195) does not accept Dean Burgon's view (*The Last Twelve Verses of St. Mark*) that they are authentic.

[3] Luke xxiv. 50, 51.                    [4] Acts i. 9–12.

posed event, must make one very chary in accepting the story; and one's doubts are increased when it is realised that such an ascension into the sky was the usual end to the mythical legends of the lives of pagan gods, just as it was to the very legendary life of Elijah.[1]  The god Adonis, whose worship flourished in the lands in which Christianity grew up, was thought to have ascended into the sky in the presence of his followers after his resurrection;[2] and, similarly, Dionysos, Herakles, Hyacinth, Krishna, Mithra, and other deities went up into heaven.

But if Jesus Christ did not at a specific moment ascend into heaven, what was His end?  Some critics suppose that He lived on in retirement, and that He was actually seen by St. Paul in that experience which is usually thought to have been only a vision, and which may have taken place as early as two or three years after the Crucifixion. In support of this theory it is to be noted that the stories, related in the Acts (A.D. 80 to 100),[3] of a

---

[1] 2 Kings ii. 11.  [2] Lucian, *De Dea Syria*, ch. 6.
[3] Acts ix. 13; xxii. 6; xxvi. 12.

vision accompanied by a dazzling light do not agree with one another, and seem therefore to be partly fictitious; while, on the other hand, St. Paul himself, writing a whole generation earlier (A.D. 52 to 64), says that he had "known Christ in the flesh,"[1] and ranks the appearance to him with those to the first disciples,[2] declaring, moreover, that he had received his instructions directly from Jesus.[3] Moreover, Suetonius states[4] that in the reign of Claudius, which began in 41 A.D., some Jews were expelled from Rome for causing a disturbance at the instigation of a certain *Chrestus*. This word *Chrestus* is generally supposed to be a miswriting for *Christus*, Christ; and it is quite possible that the meaning was that a person regarded as the Christ or Messiah was then in Rome, and that that person was Jesus Himself, this being but eleven years after the Crucifixion.

It is far more probable, however, that St. Paul's experience was in the nature of a vision, and that the last recorded appearance of Jesus in the flesh

[1] 2 Cor. v. 16; and 1 Cor. ix. 1.  [2] 1 Cor. xv. 8.
[3] 1 Cor. xi. 23.  [4] Suetonius, *Claud.*, xxv.

was no more than a few weeks after His Crucifixion; and, as I have said in the previous chapter,
the Christian of to-day is entitled to declare that
our Lord then passed away from this life, though
nobody can say when or in what manner His
passing occurred. The words "ascended into
heaven," used in the Apostles' Creed, however, are
not well chosen; for they imply that heaven is
above the clouds, an Olympus suspended in the
air above the flat earth, an old pagan idea which
surely we have outgrown.

And now, as to the Messianic prophecies.
The word *Messiah*, which the Greeks translated
as *Christos* and which we know as *Christ*, means
"The Anointed." In early times the sacred ceremony of anointing a king had the effect of making
him sacrosanct; and the kings of Israel, for example, are often spoken of as "the Lord's Anointed,"
by which is meant a sanctified ruler in close relationship with Yahweh (Jehovah). The Jewish
Messiah was thus originally conceived as an ideal
god-sent or divine king; but the idea of such a
king, who is either God incarnate or sent from

God, coming to save the nation, is found in many religions, and is not merely Jewish. For instance, the Babylonian Marduk (Merodach) was expected to come to earth as a Saviour;[1] the Mazdean religion preached the coming of the Saviour, Saoshyant, to end the dominion of Evil;[2] Krishna is described as incarnating himself for the same purpose;[3] and in Egypt there was a prophecy, dating from about 2200 B.C., which foretold the coming of a Saviour of whom it was said: "He shall be the Shepherd of his people, and in him there shall be no sin; when his flocks are scattered he shall gather them together."[4]

The idea floats through the Hebrew scriptures, but is first clearly developed in the *Book of Enoch*,[5] a compilation dating from the Second and First Centuries B.C., in which the Messiah is described as the pre-existent Son of Man who sits on the throne of God, and who shall judge the nations of the world, introducing a new heaven and a new

---

[1] Zimmern, *K.A.T.*, 3rd ed., p. 376.
[2] *Bundahish*, xi. 6.          [3] *Bhagavadgita*, iv. 5–8.
[4] Weigall, *Hist. of Pharaohs*, i., p. 284.
[5] Charles, *Book of Enoch* (English trans.).

earth. So, too, in the *Psalms of Solomon*, dating from between 70 and 40 B.C., the Messiah is clearly described as the God-sent King of the house of David, the Lord's Anointed, who shall turn the foreigners out of Jerusalem, and shall gather his holy nation together, leading them in triumph, so that all the world shall behold his glory.[1] This work is directed against the later Asmonæans (*i.e.*, Maccabees) by the Pharisees; but in the time of Jesus the Messiah was expected to release the Jews from the Roman yoke, and as the struggle with Rome became more and more imminent the hope for the arrival of this national Saviour grew ever more fervent and passionate, until there was hardly a synagogue in which it was not preached, nor a family circle in which it was not eagerly discussed. Indeed, Josephus[2] says that the final rupture with Rome was directly caused by the belief in the immediate coming of this Saviour.

The Messiah was popularly conceived as a triumphant conqueror, who should be of the royal blood of David, and should be born at

[1] *Psal. Sol.* xvii. 23–25.   [2] Josephus, *Wars*, vi. 5, sec. 4.

Bethlehem;[1] and the ordinary Jew of the time of Jesus never thought of him as anything but a deliverer from foreign oppression and a victorious King of Israel, who should establish a new dispensation wherein the Jews would be the leaders of mankind. But, quite separate from this conception of the triumphant Messiah, there was another idea of a Saviour which was preached by the great prophets of the Eighth Century B.C., but which had passed out of fashion and had been relegated to obscurity. This was the idea of a despised and rejected Servant of Yahweh, who by his sufferings should redeem the world, and should found the Kingdom of God in a spiritual sense: it took root in the Jewish mind at a time when the miseries of the nation were almost unbearable, and when the only way of facing them with equanimity was to believe that these calamities were part of God's plan for the redemption of His people. In the great Chapter LIII of Isaiah, the prophet portrays a symbolical figure of a Man of Sorrows, a personified Israel, suffering for man-

[1] Micah v. 2.

kind's transgressions; and it seems probable that this conception was the outcome of the desire to explain the nation's miseries by a resort to the world-wide belief in the efficacy of suffering.

The worship of suffering gods was to be found on all sides, and the belief in the torture of the victims in the rites of human sacrifice for the redemption from sin was very general. The gods Osiris, Attis, Adonis, Dionysos, Herakles, Prometheus, and others, had all suffered for mankind; and thus the Servant of Yahweh was also conceived as having to be wounded for men's transgressions. But, as I say, this conception had passed into the background in the days of Jesus; and when our Lord was crucified nobody, not even the disciples, thought at first that His sufferings were proof that He was the Messiah: they seemed to be proof that He was *not* the Messiah, and thus the blow was staggering.

But Jesus Himself, ever since He had realised that His mission was certain to lead to death, appears to have realised that the suffering figure was the proper conception of the Messiah; and

when He saw His disciples again after His Crucifixion He propounded the scriptures to them in
this sense,[1] and thus brought them from despair
to joyful enthusiasm. In the ensuing years they
delighted in proving to themselves how He had
fulfilled the prophecies, and they came to attribute
to Him all manner of sayings and acts which had
this significance: the fact that He had entered
Jerusalem riding on a donkey was a fulfilment of
the prophecy of Zechariah;[2] the parting of His
garments at His Crucifixion, which was a usual
custom, had been foretold in the Psalms;[3] the
giving drink to Him on the cross, again a usual
custom, had been prophesied;[4] and so forth.

But in the *Book of Enoch* and elsewhere it was
said that the Messiah would judge the nations of
the earth; and on this basis the disciples developed
the idea that Jesus would come again in glory, for,
when He left them, He had sent two messengers to
tell them that He would return. Thus they built
up the story of the Second Coming in majesty

[1] Luke xxiv. 26.
[2] Zech. ix. 9.
[3] Psalms xxii. 18.
[4] Psalms lxix. 21.

which was to bring the existing state of things to an end; and in the fervent belief that that glorious advent was imminent they prepared themselves for the supreme event, expecting it hourly, hoping against hope that this day or the morrow would bring it, gazing at the sky for the sign which never came, and searching the scriptures or their recollections of the Master's words for some prophecy which would tell them how much longer they had to wait.

# CHAPTER XI

THE recognition that Jesus had been the Messiah, and that the Messiah was not the triumphal conqueror of popular belief, but the suffering figure of the Isaiac prophecies, caused the disciples to see in the Crucifixion, which had taken place on the eve of the Passover, the supreme sacrifice for the remission of sins as exemplified in the annual Paschal sacrifice of the lamb on that day. Jesus became for them the slain Lamb of God by whose blood their transgressions were washed away: He had offered Himself up for the sins of mankind, and all the mystic lore in regard to sacrifices of sons by fathers was brought to a point in their new understanding of the Master's death on the cross and His return to life as the victor over Death. But in the process of the development of

114

this interpretation it is only natural that the minds of these first Christians should have been influenced by the religious beliefs which were then accepted in the cities and lands where they resided or whence came some of the new adherents to their faith.

Now one of the earliest seats of Christianity was Antioch; but in that city there was celebrated each year[1] the death and resurrection of the god Tammuz or Adonis, the latter name meaning simply "the Lord." This faith had always exerted its influence on Jewish thought, and, indeed, the prophet Ezekiel[2] had found it necessary to scold the women of Jerusalem for weeping for the dead Tammuz at the very gate of the Temple; while, in the end, the place at Bethlehem selected by the early Christians as the scene of the birth of Jesus (for want to any knowledge as to where the event had really occurred) was none other than an early shrine of this pagan god, as St. Jerome was horrified to discover[3]—a fact which shows that Tammuz

---

[1] Ammianus Marcellinus, xxii. 9.  [2] Ezekiel viii. 14.
[3] Jerome, *Epist.* 58, *ad Paulinum.*

or Adonis ultimately became confused in men's
minds with Jesus Christ.

This god was believed to have suffered a cruel
death, to have descended into Hell or Hades, to
have risen again, and to have ascended into
Heaven; and at his festival, as held in various
lands, his death was bewailed, an effigy of his dead
body was prepared for burial by being washed with
water and anointed, and, on the next day, his
resurrection was commemorated with great rejoicings, the very words "The Lord is risen" probably
being used. The celebration of his ascension in
the sight of his worshippers was the final act of
the festival.[1]

These ceremonies were held in some countries
in the summer, but in the neighbourhood of Palestine they appear to have taken place at about the
same time as the Passover, for Adonis was, in
certain aspects, a god of vegetation, and his resurrection denoted the revival of nature in the spring.
At Antioch, as Frazer has suggested,[2] the festival

---

[1] Lucian, *De Dea Syria*, 6; Jerome, *Comment on Ezekiel*, viii. 14.
[2] Frazer, *Adonis, Attis, Osiris*, p. 157.

seems to have been timed to coincide with the appearance of the planet Venus as the Morning Star. The whole festival, indeed, corresponded so closely with that of the death and resurrection of Jesus that the coincidence could hardly have been overlooked by the early Christians; and in certain parts of Christendom the Good Friday and Easter ceremonies of the present day appear to carry on the Adonis rites, as, for example, in Sicily and parts of Greece, where an effigy of the dead Christ is prepared for burial amidst the wailing of the people, which continues until midnight on the Saturday, when the bishop announces that the Lord is risen, and the crowds break into wild shouts of joy.

This coincidence has, of course, led many critics to suppose that the story of the burial and resurrection of Jesus is simply a myth borrowed from this pagan religion; but in the previous chapters I have tried to show that the Gospel story is, beyond doubt, historical. The Crucifixion of Jesus is related to have taken place at the time of the Passover, that is to say, at the time of the world-wide spring festivals, not because the story was taken over from paganism, but because He *was* put to death at that time in the guise of the *Bar Abbas* sacrifice, which probably took place at that date; and His resurrection is recorded as following shortly afterwards, not because Adonis and other gods were supposed to have come back to life in that manner, but because He *did* revive and come out of the tomb alive. It was, I think, largely due to this very coincidence that the Christian faith attracted such widespread attention. Had our Lord ended His ministry in some manner foreign to the generally accepted ideas of how an incarnate deity ought to have died, the belief that He was divine would not have been so quickly or so widely acknowledged.

But there is one feature of the Gospel story which seems really to have been borrowed from the Adonis religion, and, in fact, from other pagan religions also, namely, the descent into Hell. The Apostles Creed and Athanasian Creed say that between the Friday night and the Sunday morning Jesus was in Hell or Hades; but this is omitted in the Nicene Creed, and Bishop Pearson[1] has shown how frequently it was omitted in other early statements of the Faith, while Bishop Goodwin[2] feels that the article "may be put on one side." It has no scriptural foundation except in the ambiguous words of the First Epistle of Peter;[3] it did not appear in the Church as a tenet of Christianity until late in the Fourth Century;[4] and its pagan origin is shown by its appearance not only in the legend of Adonis, but in those of Herakles, Dionysos, Orpheus, Osiris, Hermes, Krishna, Balder, and other deities. In the case of Orpheus it is to be observed that his connection with Jesus in the minds of early Christians is shown by the frequency of his appearance in the paintings in the Catacombs.

Herodotus[5] describes a festival held annually in Egypt in which was commemorated the descent into Hell of a certain unidentified god or king

[1] Pearson, *On the Creed*, ii. 308.
[2] Goodwin, *Foundations of the Creed*, p. 172.
[3] 1 Pet. iii. 19; iv. 6.
[4] Nicolas, *Le Symbole des Apôtres*, pp. 221, 364.
[5] Herodotus, ii. 122.

named Rhampsinitus, and his return to earth. At this festival, which seems to have been connected with Osiris, the priests wrapped a man in a shroud and led him to the temple of Isis outside the city, where they left him, he being afterwards led back by two priests playing the parts of the two divine guides of the dead. A significant feature of this account is that the man, on his return, carried a napkin which was supposed to have been given to him in the regions below; and one is reminded thus of the story, which only occurs in the late Gospel of St. John, of how those who came to the tomb of Jesus saw the napkin lying in one place and the shroud in another, and beheld two celestial figures. This Egyptian incident has the effect of raising a doubt in regard to the napkin-story in St. John; but it is perhaps only important as an instance of the caution with which one has to examine the Gospel accounts.

Besides the worship of Adonis there were other pagan beliefs which, by their similarity, must have influenced the minds of the Gentile converts to Christianity. There was, for instance, the worship of Dionysos, but of this I will speak in Chapter XXII. Another religion which had its influence on Christianity was the worship of the Spartan god, or divine hero, Hyacinth, who had been killed by an accidental blow. His three days' festival[1] was held each year in spring or early summer: on the first day he was mourned as dead; on the second day his resurrection was celebrated with great rejoicings; and on the third day it seems that his ascension was commemorated, the sculptures at his tomb showing him ascending to heaven, with his virgin sister, in the company of angels or goddesses.

Then again, there was the worship of Attis, a very popular religion which must have influenced the early Christians. Attis was the Good Shepherd, the son of Cybele, the Great Mother, or, alternatively, of the Virgin Nana, who conceived him without union with mortal man, as in the story of the Virgin Mary; but in the prime of his manhood he mutilated himself and bled to death at the foot of his sacred pine-tree. In Rome the

[1] Frazer, *Adonis, Attis, Osiris*, pp. 178, 204.

festival of his death and resurrection[1] was annually held from March 22nd to 25th; and the connection of this religion with Christianity is shown by the fact that in Phrygia, Gaul, Italy, and other countries where Attis-worship was powerful, the Christians adopted the actual date, March 25th, as the anniversary of our Lord's passion.[2]

At this Attis festival a pine-tree was felled on March 22nd, and to its trunk an effigy of the god was fastened, Attis thus being "slain and hanged on a tree," in the Biblical phrase.[3] This effigy was later buried in a tomb. March 24th was the Day of Blood, whereon the High Priest, who himself impersonated Attis, drew blood from his arm and offered it up in place of the blood of a human sacrifice, thus, as it were, sacrificing himself, a fact which recalls to mind the words in the Epistle to the Hebrews: "Christ being come an High Priest . . . neither by the blood of goats and calves, but by his own blood . . . obtained eternal redemption for us."[4] That night the priests went

[1] See references, Frazer, *Adonis, Attis, Osiris*, p. 166, note 4.
[2] See references, Frazer, *Adonis, Attis, Osiris*, p. 199, note 3.
[3] Compare Acts v. 30.      [4] Heb. ix. 11, 12.

to the tomb and found it illuminated from within, and it was then discovered to be empty, the god having risen on the third day from the dead; and on the 25th the resurrection was celebrated with great rejoicings, a sacramental meal of some kind being taken, and initiates being baptised with blood, whereby their sins were washed away and they were said to be "born again."

There can be no doubt that these ceremonies and beliefs deeply coloured the interpretation placed by the first Christians upon the historic facts of the Crucifixion, burial, and coming again to life of Jesus; and, indeed, the merging of the worship of Attis into that of Jesus was effected almost without interruption, for these pagan ceremonies were enacted in a sanctuary on the Vatican hill, which was afterwards taken over by the Christians, and the mother church of St. Peter now stands upon the very spot.[1]

[1] Many inscriptions regarding these ceremonies have been found under St. Peter's. Hepding, *Attis*.

# CHAPTER XII

## THE INFLUENCE OF OSIRIS AND ISIS

THE popular and widespread religion of Osiris and Isis exercised considerable influence upon early Christianity, for these two great Egyptian deities, whose worship had passed into Europe, were revered in Rome and in several other centres where Christian communities were growing up. Osiris and Isis, so runs the legend,[1] were brother and sister and also husband and wife; but Osiris was murdered, his coffined body being thrown into the Nile, and shortly afterwards the widowed and exiled Isis gave birth to a son, Horus. The coffin, meanwhile, was washed up on the Syrian coast, and became miraculously lodged in the trunk of a tree, so that Osiris, like other sacrificed gods, could be described as having been "slain and hanged on a tree." This tree afterwards chanced

[1] Plutarch, *Isis and Osiris.*

124

to be cut down and made into a pillar in the palace at Byblos, and there Isis at length found it. She detached the coffin from it and mourned over it; but the tree or pillar itself she swathed in linen and placed in the temple, like the sacred tree of Attis. She then took the body of Osiris back to Egypt, where it was found by the evil powers, who tore it to pieces; but these pieces were put together again, and the god rose from the dead.[1] Afterwards, however, he returned to the other world to reign for ever as King of the Dead; and meanwhile Horus, having grown to manhood, reigned on earth, later becoming the third person of this great Egyptian trinity.

Herodotus[2] states that the festival of the death and resurrection of Osiris was held in Egypt each year, though he does not give the date; and he says that the people mourned for the dead god, and in the evening lighted lamps outside their houses which burnt all through the night. Plutarch also records the annual Osirian festival, and

---

[1] Erman, *Handbook Egy. Relig.*, p. 31.
[2] Herodotus, ii. 62.

says that it lasted four days, giving the date as the seventeenth day of the Egyptian month Hathor, which, according to the Alexandrian calendar used by him, corresponded to November 13th.[1] Now we know from old Egyptian records[2] that a feast in honour of all the dead, when such lamps were lit, was held on the eighteenth day of the first month of the year; and as the year began originally about October 21st,[3] this feast would at first have fallen on about November 8th, and thus, allowing for the adjustment of the calendar, may well be identical with that described by Herodotus.

In other words, the festival of Osiris had in ancient times become identified with the feast of lamps commemorating the dead in general, held early in November.[4] But the Christian feast of All Souls, in honour of the dead, likewise falls at the beginning of November; and in many countries lamps and candles are burnt all night on

[1] Frazer, *Adonis, Attis, Osiris*, p. 257.
[2] Breasted, *Ancient Records of Egypt*, i., sec. 555.
[3] Weigall, *History of the Pharaohs*, i., p. 20.
[4] M. Murray, *The Osireion at Abydos*, p. 35.

that occasion. This festival was first recognised by the Church in A.D. 998; but Frazer[1] has shown that by this recognition the clergy were simply regularising an immemorial and widespread pagan custom which they could not suppress, and there seems little doubt that this custom was identical with the Egyptian festival. At the Reformation the celebration was abolished in the Church of England, though it has been revived by the Anglo-Catholics; but the festival of All Saints, which is held one day before that of All Souls and which was first recognised by the Church in A.D. 835, is undoubtedly identical with it in origin. This still stands as a festival in the ecclesiastical calendar; and thus Christians unconsciously perpetuate the worship of Osiris and the commemoration of all his subjects in the Kingdom of the Dead.

The Christian Father, Firmicus Maternus,[2] writing in the Fourth Century A.D., describes how the worshippers of Osiris mourn for their dead god for a certain number of days, and then rejoice

---

[1] Frazer, *Adonis, Attis, Osiris*, p. 255.
[2] Firmicus Maternus, *De errore profanarum religionum*, ii. 3.

saying: "We have found him." In the commemoration of the god's burial, says the same
writer, the custom was to make an image of Osiris
and to place it on a pine tree which had been cut
down for the purpose; and thus, as in the case of
the god Attis, we again have the god "slain and
hanged on a tree."

But while the story of the death and resurrection
of Osiris may have influenced the thought of the
earliest Christians in regard to the death and
resurrection of our Lord, there can be no doubt
that the myths of Isis had a direct bearing upon
the elevation of Mary, the mother of Jesus, to
her celestial position in the Roman Catholic
theology.[1] The worship of Isis was introduced
into Rome in the First Century B.C., and about
80 B.C. Sulla founded an Isiac college in that city.
Soon there were temples to her at Pompeii, Bene-
vento, Malcesina on Lake Garda, and many other
places; and from the time of Vespasian onwards
her worship spread all over western Europe, some
lands being "full of the Madness of Isis," as an

[1] W. Roscher, *Lexikon griech. u. röm. Myth.*, ii. 428.

early Christian writer declares,[1] and there being a temple of Isis even in Southwark, London. In Rome the last recorded festival to her was held in A.D. 394, but her worship survived until the Fifth Century A.D., being one of the last pagan faiths to maintain itself there against Christianity.

There were two aspects of Isis which commended themselves particularly to her worshippers: firstly, that of the lady of sorrows, weeping for the dead Osiris, and, secondly, that of the divine mother, nursing her infant son, Horus. In the former capacity she was identified with the great mother-goddess, Demeter, whose mourning for Persephone was the main feature in the Eleusinian mysteries; and she was also closely related to that other Mater Dolorosa, the mother goddess Cybele, whose mourning for her dead son Attis was annually commemorated in Rome, and whose shrine stood on the Vatican hill where now stands St. Peter's, the centre of the Church which worships the "Mother of God" in just that capacity.

In her aspect as the mother of Horus, Isis was

[1] Acta SS., XX. Mai, p. 44.

represented in tens of thousands of statuettes and paintings, holding the divine child in her arms; and when Christianity triumphed these paintings and figures became those of the Madonna and Child without any break in continuity: no archæologist, in fact, can now tell whether some of these objects represent the one or the other.

Now, the title "Mother of God" was first applied to Mary, the mother of Jesus, by the theologians of Alexandria, the great Egyptian centre of Isis-worship, towards the close of the Third Century; and in the Fourth Century, when Christianity was rapidly triumphing over paganism, Mary is called by that title with increasing frequency. Shortly before A.D. 400, Epiphanius denounces the women of Thrace, Arabia, and elsewhere, for worshipping Mary as an actual goddess, and offering cakes at her shrine. About the year A.D. 430, however, the Christian theologian Proclus preached a sermon hailing her as a sort of divinity, calling her Mother of God and the mediator between God and man;[1] but to this Nestorius, another Christian

[1] Labbé, *Conc.*, iii. 51.

dignitary, objected, preferring to regard her as the earlier Christians had done, that is to say, simply as the chosen but entirely mortal vessel. In 431 Cyril of Alexandria preached a decisive sermon at Ephesus, using such terms in regard to Mary that one may regard her as having assumed the place in human affections left vacant by the fading away of Isis and of her counterpart, Diana or Artemis, who had been the great goddess of the Ephesians. As a result of this sermon, Nestorius was deposed, to the great delight of the people; and thenceforth Mary was the supreme Queen of Heaven.

At about this time a story, attributed to Melito, Bishop of Sardis in the Second Century, but probably of much later origin, began to spread that Mary had been miraculously carried to Heaven by Jesus and His angels; and in the Sixth Century the festival of the Assumption, which celebrates this event, was acknowledged by the Church,[1] and is now one of the great feasts of Roman Catholicism, though it was abandoned by the

[1] Nicephorus Callistus, *Hist. Eccles.*, xvii. 28.

Church of England at the Reformation, and is
only now gradually coming back into favour under
the auspices of the Anglo-Catholics. It is celebrated on August 13th; but that was the date of
the great festival of Diana or Artemis, with whom
Isis was identified, and one can see, thus, how
Mary had gradually taken the place of the
goddess.

Artemis was, in one aspect, identified with
Selene, the Moon-goddess, in which capacity the
crescent moon was her symbol; and Isis, similarly,
was identified with the moon. This accounts for
the presence of the crescent moon in so many
paintings of the Virgin Mary. Isis was also
identified with Venus or Aphrodite; and the mourning of Isis for the slain Osiris was thus assimilated
to the mourning of Venus for the slain Adonis.
But Aphrodite was born of the foam of the sea,
and thus Isis gradually came to be the patron
goddess of the sea, and of seamen; and when the
Madonna took the place of Isis she also took over
the title *Stella Maris*, "Star of the Sea," by which
she is so often called in Roman Catholic countries.

In this regard it is interesting to find that a figure of Isis, ship in hand, is carved upon an ivory panel of pagan times which, without any sense of incongruity, was inserted in mediæval times into the side of the ambo in the cathedral of Aix, where it may now be seen.[1]  I may mention that in the church of St. Ursula at Cologne a statue of Isis was adapted in the middle ages for one of the capitals of the pillars.[2]

Isis was also identified with the goddess Astarte, or Ashtoreth (the Ashtaroth of the Bible), Queen of Heaven; and just as we learn from Jeremiah[3] that the Hebrew women made offerings to her, so, right down to modern times at Paphos in Cyprus, the women make offerings to the Virgin Mary as Queen of Heaven in the ruins of the ancient temple of Astarte.

The festival of the Annunciation of the Blessed Virgin is celebrated in the Roman and Anglican Churches on March 25th, a date fixed by the fact

---

[1] Paul Clemen, *Kunstdenkmäler der Rheinprovinz*, 1916, x., p. 113, fig. 68.

[2] *Bonn Jahrbuch*, lxxvi. 38.   [3] Jer. xliv. 19.

that it was exactly nine months of embryogeny before December 25th, which was the date adopted by the Church as the anniversary of the birth of Jesus. But, as I shall show in another chapter, December 25th was really the date, not of the birth of Jesus, but of the sun-god, Mithra. Horus, son of Isis, however, was in very early times identified with Ra, the Egyptian sun-god,[1] and hence with Mithra; and thus the Christian festival really commemorates the Annunciation of Isis, not of Mary.

[1] Weigall, *History of the Pharaohs*, i., p. 208.

# CHAPTER XIII

## THE INFLUENCE OF MITHRA

DURING the first three and a half centuries A.D. the increasingly powerful rival of Christianity was the religion known as Mithraism, that is to say, the worship of the solar god Mithra or Mithras which had been introduced into Rome by Cilician seamen about 68 B.C., and later on spread throughout the Roman world, until, just before the final triumph of Christianity, it was the most powerful pagan faith in the Empire. It was suppressed by the Christians in A.D. 376 and 377; but its collapse seems to have been due rather to the fact that by that time many of its doctrines and ceremonies had been adopted by the Church, so that it was practically absorbed by its rival, Jesus Christ supplanting Mithra in men's worship without the need of any mental somersaults.

Originally Mithra was one of the lesser gods of

the ancient Persian pantheon, but he came to be regarded as the spiritual Sun, the heavenly Light, and the chief and also the embodiment of the seven divine spirits of goodness; and already in the time of Christ he had risen to be co-equal with, though created by, Ormuzd (Ahura-Mazda), the Supreme Being,[1] and Mediator between him and man.[2] He appears to have lived an incarnate life on earth, and in some unknown manner to have suffered death for the good of mankind, an image symbolising his resurrection being employed in his ceremonies.[3] Tarsus, the home of St. Paul, was one of the great centres of his worship, being the chief city of the Cilicians; and, as will presently appear, there is a decided tinge of Mithraism in the Epistles and Gospels. Thus the designations of our Lord as the Dayspring from on High,[4] the Light,[5] the Sun of Righteousness,[6] and similar

[1] J. M. Robertson, *Pagan Christs*, p. 290.
[2] Plutarch, *Isis et Osiris*, ch. 46; Julian, *In regem solem*, chs. 9, 10, 21.
[3] Tertullian, *Præscr.*, ch. 40.          [4] Luke i. 78.
[5] 2 Cor. iv. 6; Eph. v. 13, 14; I Thess. v. 5; etc.
[6] Malachi iv. 2; and much used in Christianity.

expressions, are borrowed from or related to Mithraic phraseology.

Mithra was born from a rock,[1] as shown in Mithraic sculptures, being sometimes termed "the god out of the rock," and his worship was always conducted in a cave; and the general belief in the early Church that Jesus was born in a cave is a direct instance of the taking over of Mithraic ideas. The words of St. Paul, "They drank of that spiritual rock . . . and that rock was Christ"[2] are borrowed from the Mithraic scriptures; for not only was Mithra "the Rock," but one of his mythological acts, which also appears in the acts of Moses, was the striking of the rock and the producing of water from it which his followers eagerly drank. Justin Martyr[3] complains that the prophetic words in the Book of Daniel[4] regarding a stone which was cut out of the rock without hands were also used in the Mithraic ritual; and it is apparent that the great importance attached by the early Church to the supposed words of

[1] Firmicus, *De errore*, xxi.; etc.  [2] 1 Cor. x. 4.
[3] Justin Martyr, *Dial. with Trypho*, ch. 70.  [4] Dan. ii. 34.

Jesus in regard to Peter—"Upon this rock I will build my church"[1]—was due to their approximation to the Mithraic idea of the *Theos ek Petras*, the "God from the Rock." Indeed, it may be that the reason of the Vatican hill at Rome being regarded as sacred to Peter, the Christian "Rock," was that it was already sacred to Mithra, for Mithraic remains have been found there.

The chief incident of Mithra's life was his struggle with a symbolical bull, which he overpowered and sacrificed, and from the blood of the sacrifice came the world's peace and plenty, typified by ears of corn. The bull appears to signify the earth or mankind, and the implication is that Mithra, like Christ, overcame the world; but in the early Persian writings Mithra is himself the bull,[2] the god thus sacrificing himself, which is a close approximation to the Christian idea. In later times the bull is interchangeable with a ram; but the zodiacal ram, Aries, which is associated with Mithra, was replaced by a lamb in the

[1] Matt. xvi. 18.
[2] J. M. Robertson, *Pagan Christs*, p. 298.

Persian zodiac,[1] so that it is a lamb which is sacrificed,[2] as in the Paschal conception of Jesus. That this sacrifice had originally a human victim, and that it later involved the idea of the sacramental death of a human being, is clear from the fact that the Church historian, Socrates, believed that human victims were still sacrificed in the Mithraic mysteries down to some period before A.D. 360.[3]

Thus the paramount Christian idea of the sacrifice of the lamb of God was one with which every worshipper of Mithra was familiar; and just as Mithra was an embodiment of the seven spirits of God, so the slain Lamb in the Book of Revelation has seven horns and seven eyes "which are the seven spirits of God."[4] Early writers say that a lamb was consecrated, killed, and eaten as an Easter rite in the Church; but Easter was a Mithraic festival,[5] presumably of the resurrection of their god, and the parallel is thus complete, in

[1] Bundahish, ii. 2.
[2] Garucci, *Les Mystères du Syn. Phrygien*, p. 34.
[3] Socrates, *Eccles. Hist.*, bk. iii., ch. 2.
[4] Rev. v. 6.  [5] Macrobius, *Saturnalia*, i. 18.

which regard it is to be noted that in the Seventh
Century the Church endeavoured without success
to suppress the picturing of Christ as a lamb,
owing to the paganism involved in the idea.[1]

The ceremonies of purification by the sprinkling
or drenching of the novice with the blood of bulls
or rams were widespread, and were to be found in
the rites of Mithra. By this purification a man
was "born again,"[2] and the Christian expression
"washed in the blood of the Lamb" is undoubtedly
a reflection of this idea, the reference thus being
clear in the words of the Epistle to the Hebrews:
"It is not possible that the blood of bulls and of
goats should take away sins." In this passage the
writer goes on to say: "Having boldness to enter
into the holiest by the blood of Jesus, by a new
and living way which he hath consecrated for us
through the veil, that is to say his flesh . . . let
us draw near . . . having our hearts sprinkled
from an evil conscience, and our bodies washed
with pure water."[3] But when we learn that the

[1] Bingham, *Christian Antiq.*, viii. 8, sec. 11; xv. 2, sec. 3.
[2] Beugnot, *Hist. de la Destr. du Paganisme*, i. p. 334.
[3] Heb. x. 19.

Mithraic initiation ceremony consisted in entering boldly into a mysterious underground "holy of holies," with the eyes veiled, and there being sprinkled with blood, and washed with water, it is clear that the author of the Epistle was thinking of those Mithraic rites with which everybody at that time must have been so familiar.

Another ceremony in the religion of Mithra was that of stepping across a channel of water, the hands being entangled in the entrails of a bird, signifying sin, and of being "liberated" on the other side; and this seems to be referred to by St. Paul when he says: "Stand fast in the liberty wherewith Christ has made us free, and be not entangled again with the yoke of bondage."[1]

Tertullian[2] states that the worshippers of Mithra practised baptism by water, through which they were thought to be redeemed from sin, and that the priest made a sign upon the forehead of the person baptised; but as this was also a Christian rite, Tertullian declares that the Devil must have effected the coincidence for his wicked

---

[1] Gal. v. 1.    [2] Tertullian, *Præscr.*, ch. 40.

ends. "The Devil," he also writes, "imitates even the main parts of our divine mysteries," and "has gone about to apply to the worship of idols those very things of which the administration of Christ's sacraments consists."

In this he must be referring both to the baptismal rite and also to the Mithraic eucharist, of which Justin Martyr[1] had already complained when he declared that it was Satan who had plagiarised the ceremony, causing the worshippers of Mithra to receive the consecrated bread and cup of water. The ceremony of eating an incarnate god's body and drinking his blood is, of course, of very ancient, and originally cannibalistic, inception, and there are several sources from which the Christian rite may be derived if, as most critics think, it was not instituted as an actual ceremony by Jesus; but its connection with the Mithraic rite is the most apparent.

The worshippers of Mithra were called "Soldiers of Mithra," which is probably the origin of the term "Soldiers of Christ" and of the exhortation to

[1] Justin Martyr, 1 *Apol.*, ch. 66.

Christians to "put on the armour of light,"[1]
Mithra being the god of Light. As in Christianity,
they recognised no social distinctions, both rich
and poor, freemen and slaves, being admitted into
the Army of the Lord. Mithraism had its aus-
terities, typified in the severe initiation rites endured by a "Soldier of Mithra"; and the Epistle
to Timothy, similarly, exhorts the Christian to
"endure hardness as a good soldier of Jesus
Christ."[2] It had also its nuns and its male
celibates;[3] and one of its main tenets was the
control of the flesh and the repudiation of the
world, this being symbolised in the initiation ceremony, whereat a crown was offered to the novice,
who had to reject it, saying, as did the Christians,
that it was to a heavenly crown that he looked.
We hear, too, of hymns which could be used with
equal propriety by Christians and Mithraists
alike.[4]

The Mithraic worship always took place in

[1] Rom. xiii. 12. Compare also Eph. vi. 11, 13.
[2] 2 Tim. ii. 3.                [3] Tertullian, *Præscr.*, ch. 40.
[4] *Rev. Arch.*, vol. xvii. (1911), p. 397.

caves, these being either natural or artificial. Now the early Christians, openly and for no reasons of secrecy or security, employed those subterranean rock chambers known as catacombs both for their burials and for public worship. Like the Mithraic caves, these catacombs were decorated with paintings, amongst which the subject of Moses striking the rock, which, as I have said above, has a Mithraic parallel, is often represented. The most frequent theme is that of Christ as the Good Shepherd; and although it is generally agreed that the figure of Jesus carrying a lamb is taken from the statues of Hermes Kriophoros,[1] the kid-carrying god, Mithra is sometimes shown carrying a bull across his shoulders, and Apollo, who, in his solar aspect and as the patron of the rocks,[2] is to be identified with Mithra, is often called "the Good Shepherd." At the birth of Mithra the child was adored by shepherds, who brought gifts to him.[3]

[1] Pausanias, iv. 33.   [2] *Hymn to the Delian Apollo.*
[3] *Encyc. Brit.*, 11th ed., vol. xvii., p. 623.

# THE INFLUENCE OF MITHRA

The Hebrew Sabbath having been abolished by Christians, the Church made a sacred day of Sunday, partly because it was the day of the resurrection, but largely because it was the weekly festival of the sun; for it was a definite Christian policy to take over the pagan festivals endeared to the people by tradition, and to give them a Christian significance. But, as a solar festival, Sunday was the sacred day of Mithra; and it is interesting to notice that since Mithra was addressed as *Dominus*, "Lord," Sunday must have been "the Lord's Day" long before Christian times. I may again mention here, in passing, a subject to which I have already referred and will return in a later chapter, namely, that of the origin of our Christmas. December 25th was the birthday of the sun-god, and particularly of Mithra, and was only taken over in the Fourth Century as the date, actually unknown, of the birth of Jesus.

The head of the Mithraic faith was called *Pater Patrum*, "Father of the Fathers," and was seated at Rome; and similarly the head of the Church was the *Papa*, or "Father," now known as the Pope, who was also seated at Rome. The Pope's crown is called a tiara, but a tiara is a Persian, and hence perhaps a Mithraic, headdress. The ancient chair preserved in the Vatican and supposed to have been the pontifical throne used by St. Peter is in reality of pagan origin, and may possibly be Mithraic also, for it has upon it certain pagan carvings which are thought to be connected with Mithra.[1]

[1] J. M. Robertson, *Pagan Christs*, p. 336.

# CHAPTER XIV

## THE ORIGIN OF THE EUCHARIST

In the previous chapter I pointed out that a sacramental eucharist was a feature of the rites of Mithraism; and the reader will recall that the elements were bread and water, not bread and wine. I want now to show that in the First Century the Christian celebration was simply a ceremony of "remembrance" forming part of a real meal, the second element in those days being wine; but that in the Second Century the ceremony became a sacrament, and at the same time water took the place of wine, which seems to show that the Mithraic rite influenced the Christian.

The earliest known reference to the Christian ceremony is that in St. Paul's First Epistle to the Corinthians,[1] written some five-and-twenty years

[1] 1 Cor. xi. 17–34.

after the Crucifixion. Here we are told that the faithful were wont to meet and to celebrate the Lord's Supper by eating a meal together, apparently from a common stock of provisions, but that this had degenerated into an unseemly affair in which some ate and drank too much or too quickly, and others did not get enough. St. Paul therefore enjoins them to restrain themselves and to wait for one another, adding that since this is a sacred meal, in which the body of Jesus is to be discerned, those who are hungry should have something to eat at home before coming. He then reminds them of the origin of the ceremony, which he relates thus: "The Lord Jesus on the night in which he was betrayed took bread, and having given thanks brake it and said, This is my body which is broken for your sake; this do in remembrance of me. In like manner also the cup, after supper, saying, This cup is the new covenant through my blood; this do, as oft as ye drink it, in remembrance of me."

Elsewhere in the same Epistle[1] he says: "The

---

[1] I Cor. x. 16–31

cup of blessing which we bless, is it not the communion of the blood of Christ? The bread which
we break, is it not the communion of the body
of Christ?" And he warns the Corinthians against
participating in similar ceremonies in honour of
pagan gods, whom he describes as "devils": "Ye
cannot drink the cup of the Lord," he says, "and
the cup of devils; ye cannot be partakers of the
Lord's Table, and of the table of devils. Do we
(want to) provoke the Lord to jealousy?" The
meal, thus, was a sacred rite, akin to certain
sacred rites in other religions, and perhaps copied
to some extent from the Kiddûsh, the religious
meal partaken of by the Jews on the eve of the
Sabbath, at which the bread and the cup were
solemnly blessed; and while there is an indication[1]
that all present partook of the broken fragments of
one loaf of blessed bread, and that the meal ended[2]
in the handing round of a special cup of wine, the
general character of the ceremony was that of a
communal dinner. So it remained as late as
A.D. 112, when, in the famous letter written by

[1] Verse 17.     [2] Note the words "after supper."

Pliny,[1] the meal is described as being classed with those of other societies (or trade-guilds), and as being quite ordinary and innocent. Probably it was much like the sacred feasts held in the temple of Serapis at Alexandria, which, according to Aristides, established a real communion with the god. An invitation to one of these feasts of Serapis has been found in modern times in Egypt.[2]

In the *Didache*,[3] or *Teaching of the Apostles*, a document which dates from some time soon after A.D. 90, instructions are given in regard to this meal which, we there learn, was held on Sundays. The proceedings were opened by the handing round of the cup, the contents of which were described simply as "the holy wine of David," no reference being made to Christ's blood; and then the broken bread was distributed, it being described as symbolical of "the life and knowledge made known to us through Jesus." Thereafter the company ate heartily of the common provi-

---

[1] Letter xcviii. Its authenticity is not seriously in doubt.
[2] Grenfell and Hunt, *Pap. Ox.*, i. 110.
[3] J. E. Odgers, *Didache* (English trans.), chs. ix. x.

sions, and "after being filled" gave thanks for the actual food and drink given by God for men's enjoyment, and also for the spiritual food and drink and for the life eternal made known through Jesus. In the Gospel of St. Mark,[1] dating from about the same time, the account of the incident in the life of Jesus upon which the ceremony was founded is given in much the same words as those of St. Paul, but with this difference, that in reference to the cup He says: "This is my blood of the new covenant, which is shed for many." In the next Gospel, that of St. Luke,[2] the account is very similar.

From these two Gospel stories the incident can be reconstructed. It was the evening of Thursday, the actual date perhaps being April 6th, A.D. 30;[3] and the company was gathered to eat the traditional Passover meal. Jesus knew that He was liable to be arrested at any moment, and that His execution would follow as a matter of course;

---

[1] Mark xiv. 22–25.  [2] Luke xxii. 19, 20.

[3] If the year was A.D. 30, the date was April 6th; but it is not certain that this is the correct year. The whole subject may be most conveniently studied in the *Encyc. Brit.* under "Bible."

and therefore when, in the usual manner of a host, He handed round the pieces of bread to be dipped as sops into the gravy of the cooked lamb, He made the sad remark that even so His body would be broken.  And later on, after the meal, when, as was customary, He handed round the cup of wine, He likened it to His blood which was to be shed, and asked His friends not to forget the sacrifice He was making, but to remember His death whenever they broke bread or drank wine.

There is no authentic evidence that Jesus ever intended to establish a Church or to lay down any rules for future ecclesiastical rites.  He was opposed to forms and ceremonies, the Kingdom of Heaven which he preached being in men's hearts; and thus it is not surprising to find that the Christians of the First Century commemorated the incident only in the manner described above. But now a change took place in the ceremony.  In the Gospel of St. John (perhaps about A.D. 105) the incident of the Last Supper is deliberately omitted, as though it were not a sufficient foundation for the new sacramentalism which was attaching itself to the rite, and, instead, a long passage[1] is put in, purporting to give the words of Jesus. Here He is supposed to say that He is the bread of life, the living bread; that His flesh is meat indeed, and His blood drink indeed; and that unless men eat His flesh and drink His blood they shall not have eternal life. This Gospel, in fact, which was not recognised as authoritative by the early Church, is the only one wherein Jesus is spoken of as "bread" or "water" at all. Then comes the latest Synoptic Gospel, that of St. Matthew[2] (A.D. 100–110), in which, after the words "This is my blood of the new covenant which is shed for many," somebody has added "for the remission of sins," an acknowledged interpolation, giving a sacrificial interpretation to the passage.

Now at about the same time that the original communal meal and "remembrance ceremony" was changed into a sacramental rite, water was substituted for wine; and Justin Martyr,[3] writing

---

[1] John vi. 48–58.      [2] Matt. xxvi. 28.
[3] Justin Martyr, 1 *Apol.*, ch. 65.

about A.D. 140, describes how the faithful now receive the bread and water[1] distributed by the deacons, and how these elements are regarded as the flesh and blood of Jesus. He then adds that bread and water are also used in the eucharist of the Mithra-worshippers, a fact which he attributes to the machinations of Satan; and in regard to the bread it is significant that it was made up in the form of wafers, each marked with a cross, as is to be seen in a bas-relief representing a Mithraic communion, discovered in modern times.[2] For some years water was used instead of wine in many Christian communities, but Irenæus (about A.D. 180) speaks of water mixed with wine, and this usage may have led to an interpolation in the Gospel of St. John of the statement that mixed blood and water had flowed from the pierced side of Jesus.[3] Plain water, however, was still in use as late as A.D. 250; but at the time of the suppression of paganism at the end of the Fourth Century

[1] The Codex Othobonianus mentions bread and water only, but in other texts "wine" has been interpolated.

[2] Photo. in Cumont, *Les Mystères de Mithra*.

[3] John xix. 34.

it was forbidden by law—a further indication that its use had been borrowed from pagan rites. I may add that some critics suppose the Mithraic eucharist to have commemorated the "last supper" of Mithra when he ate the meal with Helios before ascending to heaven.[1]

These facts show clearly, I think, that the Lord's Supper had been changed from an actual meal into a sacramental rite under Mithraic and other ancient influences; and therefore we must look for the origin of its new sacrificial character in the older religions. In primitive days cannibalism had been very widely practised for the purpose of acquiring the virtues of the dead person by eating his flesh and drinking his blood. It was customary to eat the flesh of a sacrificial victim, either human or animal, and in the cases in which such victims were identified with the deity to whom they were offered, the flesh was eaten and the blood drunk in order to effect communion with the divinity. Actual cannibalism had not wholly died out in the civilised world in the First

[1] *Encyc. Brit.*, 11th ed., vol. xvii., p. 624.

Century A.D., and rites which were a palpable substitution for it were practised on all sides, as in the case of the mysteries of Dionysos, at which the baked image of a child was eaten, and those of Apollo at Larissa, where the oracle was delivered by a priestess who used to drink the blood of the sacrificed lamb and so become possessed by the god. Tertullian, writing about A.D. 200, says that human blood was still drunk in the worship of the Latiarian Jove.[1] The early Christians, in fact, must thus have been quite familiar with the idea of the sacramental eating of a god's body; and, indeed, one may say that such phrases as "Except ye eat the flesh of the Son of Man and drink his blood . . ." could only have been written by one who had been brought up amongst rites based on an immemorial cannibalism and to whom the idea of devouring his god was perfectly normal.

Having once become paganised in this manner the Christian rite took on a definitely cannibalistic character; and the idea of transubstantiation, by

[1] Tertullian, *Adv. Gnosticos*, 7.

which the bread and wine were thought to become the actual body and blood of Jesus, developed apace. Tertullian says that the priests took great care that no crumb of bread or drop of water should fall to the ground, lest the body of Jesus should be hurt. Soon it became customary in certain Christian communities to arrange the bread in the form of a man, so that one communicant should eat Christ's ear, another His eye, a third His finger, and so on, according to their social rank, this being forbidden at length by Pope Pelagius I. In 818 Paschasius was much troubled by the thought that Christ's body, having been eaten, might be turned into excrement; and in the Middle Ages there were serious arguments as to what should be done if a person were to vomit after receiving the sacrament, or if a dog or mouse were by chance to eat God's body.[1] In the Ninth Century Hincmar of Reims affirmed that the only reason why the sacramental bread still had the appearance of bread after being mystically

---

[1] A. Walker, *Popery*, 2nd ed., p. 174.    See also *Encyc. Brit.*, "Eucharist," etc.

changed into the flesh of Jesus, was that God had realised how dreadful it would be for the communicant if the real flesh, raw and bloody, were to become visible.

In the bull of Pius IV, issued after the Council of Trent, the Roman Catholic dogma in regard to transubstantiation was stated thus: "In the sacrament of the Eucharist there is truly, really, and in substance the body and blood, together with the soul and divinity, of our Lord Jesus Christ; and there does take place a conversion of the entire substance of the bread into the body, and of the entire substance of the wine into the blood;[1] and in the Helvetic Confession[2] of 1566 it is stated that at the Eucharist "there is a sacramental chewing of the Lord's body." But at the Reformation the English Church adopted the view that "the body of Christ is eaten only after a spiritual manner," and it rejected transubstantiation as idolatrous, giving strict injunctions in regard to the reservation of the sacrament in case it should

[1] *Conc. Trid. Sess.*, xiii., c. iv., etc.
[2] *Caput* XXI., *De sacra cœna Domini.*

be worshipped in the Roman manner as the actual body of our Lord.[1]

The ancient pagan idea, however, which, as has been shown above, passed into the Church in the Second Century, is gradually coming back into the Anglican rite; for the old gods die slowly, and the cannibal instincts of the human race are still latent in its mysticism. But the Protestants in their fight with the Anglo-Catholics in regard to this matter believe that they are opposing themselves to Popish practices: they do not seem to realise that actually they are defending a sort of rationalism of the Twentieth Century against the immemorial traditions of the whole ancient and pagan world.

[1] *Articles of Religion* in the Prayer Book.

# CHAPTER XV

THE doctrine of the Atonement has been regarded
for so long as the very centre of the Christian
faith that the tendency to reconsider its significance, which is apparent in intellectual Christian circles, comes as a shock to the conservative.
Yet it does not actually appear as a dogma in
the ordinary "Apostles' Creed" except in so far
as the words "the forgiveness of sins" involves it;
and in the "Athanasian Creed," recited in the
Church of England on certain feasts, the words
"Christ, who suffered for our salvation" are the
only reference to it. In the seldom read Thirty-
nine Articles of the Anglican Faith, however, the
words are definite: "Christ suffered to reconcile
his Father to us, and to be a sacrifice, not only for
original guilt, but also for all actual sins of men;"
and "the offering of Christ once made is that
perfect redemption, propitiation, and satisfaction

for all the sins of the whole world, both original and actual, and there is none other satisfaction for sin, but that alone."

The doctrine as it is understood by conservative Christians is simply this: Owing to the disobedience of Adam in eating the symbolical apple which God had forbidden him to eat, sin and death entered the world, and every human being was henceforth born under a curse and was debarred from heaven's bliss, except in certain privileged cases. God, however, wishing at last to end this situation and to restore normal relations with mankind, sent His Son into the world so that He might suffer a sacrificial death which could be regarded by the Creator as full satisfaction for Adam's crime; and the result has been that the Christian is not now prevented by Original Sin from entering heaven. This restoration of normal relations between God and man is the "at-one-ment" (the original meaning of atonement), that is to say, the great reconciliation, and it was thus brought about by the propitiatory value of the sufferings and death of Jesus.

It should be explained at the outset that in these days, when the recognition of the descent of man from lower forms of life has eliminated Adam and Eve from history, and has relegated them to the province of mythological legend, our ideas of Original Sin have had to be adjusted. By this term the Christian now means the tendency of every man towards sinfulness, due to his animal or lower nature. This adjustment, however, is very easily made; and no man, however much he may smile at the absurdity of the legend of the Garden of Eden, will deny that he enters upon life with a load of potential evil upon his shoulders which may still very fittingly be described as Original Sin.

In that respect modern thought does not clash with primitive Christian ideas; but in regard to the propitiation for these evil inclinations the case is different. We can no longer accept the appalling theological doctrine that for some mystic reason a propitiatory sacrifice was necessary. It outrages either our conception of God as almighty or else our conception of Him as all-loving. The

famous Dr. Cruden[1] believed that for the purposes
of this sacrifice "Christ suffered dreadful pains inflicted by God"; and this, of course, is a stand-
point which nauseates the modern mind, and
which may well be termed a hideous doctrine, not
unconnected with the sadistic tendencies of primitive human nature.

Actually, it is of pagan origin, being indeed
perhaps the most obvious relic of heathendom in
the Faith; and, as I shall show in the next chapter,
it is not, of course, supported by anything known
to have been said by Jesus Himself. In the
ancient world there was a very widespread belief
in the sufferings and deaths of gods as being beneficial to man. Adonis, Attis, Dionysos, Herakles,
Mithra, Osiris, and other deities, were all saviour-
gods whose deaths were regarded as sacrifices
made on behalf of mankind; and it is to be noticed
that in almost every case there is clear evidence
that the god sacrificed himself to himself.

In general this idea of a god dying for the benefit of mankind, and rising again, had its origin in

[1] Cruden, *Concordance.*

the fact that nature seemed to die in winter and revive in spring, this phenomenon leading to the supposition that death was necessary to life, and hence that the god concerned must needs die to insure his own life's revival in the growing of the crops. Human sacrifices were a feature of many early religions, and there is much to show that the person slain was regarded for the purpose as identical with the god to whom he was sacrificed: for instance, the executioner was sometimes formally chased away or ritually abused after killing the victim, which shows that the latter was regarded as holy. Moreover, in these human sacrifices there was often an elaborate and gruesome pretence that the victim, in the divine manner, was offering himself of his own free will, his struggles being prevented either by the administration of a drug or else by the breaking of his legs and arms.

The central idea in the worship of Adonis was the death and resurrection of this god: he was killed by a boar, but the boar was an incarnation of himself, and thus the god was both executioner and victim, an idea propounded in the Epistle to

the Hebrews,[1] wherein Christ is described as the
High Priest who, to put away sin, sacrificed Himself. Similarly, Mithra sacrificed a bull, but this
bull, again, was himself; a goat and bull were
sacrificed to Dionysos, but they were themselves
aspects of that god; a bear was sacrificed to
Artemis, but this bear, likewise, was Artemis her-
self; and so forth. In the *Havamal* a magic rune
is given, referring to a sacrifice to the god Odin,
reading: "I know that I hung on the windy tree
for nine whole nights, wounded with the spear,
dedicated to Odin, myself to myself."[2] Attis
mutilated himself and died; but he was the Father-
god as well as the sacrificed Son.

Thus the idea of a god atoning to himself for
the sins of mankind by his own sacrifice was
widespread; and human sacrifices in general,
directly or indirectly symbolising the beneficial
deaths of gods, were matters of ordinary thought
and conversation. Tertullian says that children
were sacrificed to Saturn as late as the proconsul-

[1] Heb. ix. 11, 26, 28.
[2] Frazer, *Adonis, Attis, Osiris*, bk. ii., ch. v.

ship of Tiberius,[1] Dion Cassius speaks of the
sacrifice of two soldiers to Mars in the time of
Julius Cæsar;[2] and other instances might be cited
to show how general was the belief in the efficacy
of human sacrifice in the time of Christ. The
idea was not repugnant to the Jews: the barbaric
story of how Abraham was about to sacrifice his
own son caused no shudder; the various hangings
before the Lord, such as those of the seven princes
at the time of the barley harvest,[3] were looked
upon as perfectly normal occurrences; and the
Barabbas sacrifice, discussed in Chapter VII,
seems to have been an accepted custom.

In the famous fifty-third chapter of Isaiah the
prophet had developed the idea of a national
figure, distinct from the Messiah, who, by his
sufferings and death, should atone for the sins
of the nation; and in later Judaism great stress
was laid on the idea that Israel made atonement
for its iniquities by the blood of the righteous.
No orthodox Jew, of course, ever thought that

---

[1] Tertullian, *Apologeticus*, ix.
[2] Dion Cassius, xlii. 24.          [3] 2 Samuel xxi. 9.

the promised Messiah would have to suffer: he was to be a conquering hero and divine leader; but it was the common opinion that the sufferings of the nation and the deaths of its innocent saints were propitiations for sin, and, indeed, that a righteous people must perforce be a suffering people.

The immemorial Jewish views as to sin-offerings were firmly held in the time of Christ: the sacrifice of a lamb, goat, or some other animal for the remission of sins was a regular custom, and the scapegoat, which, bearing all the sins of the nation, was driven into the wilderness to be devoured by beasts of prey, was employed as a variant for this practice. "The life of the flesh is in the blood," said the fearful old words of the Law,[1] "and I have given it to you upon the altar to make an atonement for your souls, for it is the blood that maketh atonement for the soul." And at the time when Jesus preached His message of love and gentleness, not only was the Jewish mind full of these thoughts of sacrificial butchery, but on all sides the pagan

[1] Lev. xvii. 11.

gods were supposed to have suffered and bled for mankind, while their altars reeked with the blood of human and animal victims tortured and slain for the remission of sins. Thus the first Christians were very open to accept such an explanation of the death of Jesus, and no sooner had they realised that it was the Messiah Himself who was to suffer torture and death as a propitiatory sacrifice for sin than the degradation of the calamity which had overtaken the Master was changed to a sacramental triumph.

This was the Lamb of God, slain that His blood might take away the sins of the world; this was the greatest of all those traditional sacrifices of royal sons by their royal fathers; this was the supreme instance of the deity on earth sacrificing Himself to His counterpart in Heaven! The fact that Jesus had been crucified at the time of the Passover clinched the matter: He was to the Jewish converts the Paschal offering without blemish. And to the Gentile proselytes He was the eternally youthful Adonis, killed by the boar who was himself; He was the bull of Mithra killed by the god who was himself; He was Herakles offering himself up in the sacrificial fire; He was Prometheus bound to the rock; He was Attis mutilating his own body; He was the High Priest sacrificing Himself to the God from whom he emanated, for a sin-offering; He was the Son sacrificed by the Father for the redemption of the nation from the avenging demons.[1]

The sacrificial nature of the Crucifixion, the sacramental value of the Passion, became astonishingly plain; but this interpretation would not have been so immediately apparent had not there been these prehistoric beliefs to prepare the mind for the revelation. Jesus not only fulfilled the Judaic scriptures, but He also fulfilled those of the pagan world; and therein lay the great appeal of early Christianity. In Him a dozen shadowy gods were condensed into a proximate reality; and in His Crucifixion the old stories of their ghastly atoning sufferings and sacrificial deaths were made actual, and were given a direct meaning.

It is not to be wondered at, then, that the dark

[1] See Chapter VII.

and savage doctrine of the Atonement became the central dogma of the new Faith: it is only a matter of astonishment that it is still preached in the Twentieth Century.

# CHAPTER XVI

## THE DEVELOPMENT OF THE DOCTRINE OF THE ATONEMENT

In the last chapter I showed that the idea of a propitiatory sacrifice as an explanation of the "scandal" of the cross presented itself to the minds of the earliest Christians owing to the fact that both in Judaism and in many pagan faiths such an idea was already well known. The sacrificial sufferings and deaths of gods on behalf of mankind, let me repeat, were commonplaces of pagan theology; and though the Jews had never thought of the Messiah as one who would have to suffer, they believed that the sufferings of representatives of Israel in atonement for sin were demanded by the scriptures. Therefore, as I said before, as soon as the Jewish followers of Jesus Christ came to understand that the ignoble death of their Master was in accord with the Messianic prophecies and had carried into effect the traditional idea of an atoning sacrifice, their belief in His divinity was gloriously confirmed; and, since such an atonement was so well understood by pagans also, the Gentile converts found in it the most convincing factor in the whole argument.

Now, Jesus Himself had never said anything which could be interpreted with certainty as meaning that the forgiveness of original or actual sin, and a great reconciliation between God and man, were to be the consequences of His death; He had never said that His death was to be regarded as a sacrificial atonement. The words "the Son of Man came . . . to give his life a ransom for many"[1] are evidently a comment of the author of the Gospel, and not the words of Jesus; and even if spoken by Jesus they might only have meant that just as He had lived to bring happiness to others, so He was prepared to die alone for His cause without implicating His followers.

The words used by Him at the Last Supper are

[1] Mark x. 45.

usually supposed to indicate the sacrificial and atoning nature of His death; but this is a misinterpretation. In the Gospel of St. Mark Jesus says: "This is my blood of the new covenant which is shed for many," and in St. Luke He says "This cup is the new covenant in my blood, which is shed for you"; and it is only in the much later Gospel of St. Matthew that the words "for the remission of sins" are added. "The most conservative critic," writes the late Dean of Carlisle, "will have no hesitation in treating this addition as an explanatory gloss by the author of the Gospel";[1] and the meaning of the other words may well have been simply that He was about to lay down His life for His friends and to die for the cause.

The real and historic Jesus never bothered Himself about the mysteries of theology: His life was one of transparent simplicity, and the basis of His teaching was that God was the loving Father who would pardon sin upon the sole condition of true repentance. He would have been appalled, one may well suppose, at the sug-

[1] H. Rashdall, *The Idea of Atonement.*

gestion that God had not been loving towards men, but had shown implacable anger against them which could only be mollified by the torture and ignoble execution of the Messiah. But St. Paul had a theological mind, and having been convinced by those from whom he had learnt the faith,[1] that Jesus had died to atone sacrificially for men's wickedness, he developed the idea with enthusiasm.

He did not press the doctrine that the death of an innocent victim had turned God's wrath away, but he put forward the view that "God was in Christ reconciling the world unto himself"[2] —a statement diametrically opposed to that in the Anglican Thirty-nine Articles, where it is said that "Christ suffered to reconcile his Father to us." Yet the idea of a sacrifice was certainly in his mind, for he writes: "God sent his Son as an offering for sin"; "Our Passover also hath been sacrificed, even Christ"; "We are justified (*i.e.*, acquitted) by his blood"; and so on. It is a question whether the Epistle to the Ephesians

[1] 1 Cor. xv. 3.  [2] 2 Cor. v. 19.

is a genuine Pauline letter, but we have there the definite doctrine that Jesus Christ "gave himself up for us, an offering and a sacrifice to God for an odour of a sweet smell."[1]

The Epistle to the Hebrews, which was written, it is agreed, by an unknown author and not by St. Paul, emphasises the sacrificial nature of the Passion. Jesus is said to have put away sin by the sacrifice of Himself: He is the High Priest slaughtering Himself, because the law said that without the shedding of blood there could be no remission of sins, and now, for the final expiation, the most precious victim of all was required. He had to "taste death on behalf of every man"; He had to make "propitiation for the sins of the people"; He had "to put away sin by the sacrifice of Himself"; He had "to obtain eternal redemption for us neither by the blood of goats and calves, but by his own blood."

The First Epistle of St. Peter lays great stress on the sufferings involved in the sacrifice, and on the efficacy of the blood. The Christians are

[1] Eph. v. 2.

elected "unto obedience and sprinkling of the blood of Jesus Christ," and they are "redeemed with the precious blood of Christ, as of a lamb without blemish," "who bare our sins in His own body on the tree."[1]

In complete contrast, however, to the Petrine and Pauline writings is the Epistle of St. James, which gives more quotations from or allusions to the teaching of Jesus than do any of the other epistles, and which breathes the very spirit of the Master. No reference is made to the sacrifice of His Crucifixion; and for that reason those who believe strongly in the Atonement regard it with disfavour: Luther, in fact, called it an "epistle of straw."

The Book of Revelation, of course, is full of the sacrificial idea. Christ "loosed us from our sins by his blood," and has "purchased unto God by his blood men of every nation"; and praise of the sacrificed Lamb rings through the whole tremendous composition. And in the Gospel of St. John, which belongs to the same school of thought,

[1] I Pet. ii. 24.

# THE DOCTRINE OF THE ATONEMENT

Jesus is called "the Lamb of God which taketh away the sins of the world."

Now in all the books of the New Testament it is assumed that the death of Jesus was a necessity, but nowhere are we told how this necessity came about or in what manner His death has operated on behalf of sinners; for the statement that His sacrifice reconciled man to God, and paid the price of sin, leaves in the mind a further "Why?" and "How?" The various authors of the canonical books, in fact, were so accustomed to the pre-Christian ideas of an expiatory sacrifice and atonement that they accepted it without going to the roots of the matter. But this vagueness was not to the liking of the early Christian Fathers. In the Second Century A.D. Irenæus, and after him other writers, explained the doctrine by what is called the "Ransom Theory," which states that the Devil was lawful lord of mankind owing to Adam's fall, and that God, being unable with justice to take Satan's subjects from him without paying a ransom for them, handed over His own incarnate Son in exchange. Satan thereupon brought about the death upon the cross, only to find that God had tricked him; for Christ was immortal and flew off back to heaven.[1]

This remained the orthodox explanation of the death of Jesus Christ for nearly a thousand years, until Anselm, Archbishop of Canterbury (1093), and Abelard, a few years later, had the courage to deny that Satan ever had any lawful rights over mankind which God had been obliged to respect. Abelard paid for his temerity by being condemned to perpetual imprisonment; yet his teachings prevailed, and the theory of a bargain with the Devil, and of the trick God played upon him, passed out of fashion.

This threw the Church back upon the Augustine theory that all men were doomed by God to eternal torments, but that Jesus Christ had asked His Father to let Him die in their stead, whereupon God had accepted this death as more than equivalent in value to those of all mankind, and had exonerated them from the previously unavoidable fate of everlasting damnation. The views of Roman

[1] H. Rashdall, *The Idea of Atonement*, p. 248.

# THE DOCTRINE OF THE ATONEMENT

Catholics and Protestants have remained fairly similar in regard to the matter; but Luther and some of the reformers were very emphatic about it all, and declared that Christ "really and truly offered Himself to the Father for eternal punishment on our behalf." Nowadays the teaching of the Salvation Army is perhaps the most blatant in its interpretation of the Passion as a propitiatory sacrifice; and the idea of sinners being sprinkled with, or washed in, the blood of the slain victim, and thus purged of their sins, still leads to as much emotional frenzy as it did in the case of the Taurobolium, where the worshippers of Cybele were washed in the blood of a sacrificed bull, and were thus said to be "born again," or in the case of the Mithra rites, where a similar blood-bath was a feature of the initiation ceremony.

Advanced Christian thinkers now regard the Crucifixion of our Lord as the supreme sacrifice made by Him for the sake of the principles of His teaching. It was the crowning act of His most heroic life, and it affords such a sublime example to mankind that meditation upon it may be said to produce a condition of at-one-ment with the Fountain-head of all goodness. The tendency is to repudiate the earlier doctrine of a sacrificial atonement as being too obviously connected with barbarous and prehistoric beliefs; but the human taste for blood and for sacrificial mysteries is very persistent, and hence it may be feared that the Doctrine of the Atonement will be yet preached for many years to come. It is part and parcel of Christian theology, but, by that very token, it has nothing to do with the historic Jesus.

# CHAPTER XVII

## THE DIVINITY OF JESUS

IT was at the Council of Nicæa in the year 325, that is to say, about three centuries after the Crucifixion, that Jesus was first recognised officially by the Church as God. Previous to that He had not been generally regarded by Christians as an actual deity. True, the idea, implicit in the early theory of His atoning sacrifice, that He had offered Himself to Himself, linked Him with the Supreme Being in an inseparable union; but the thought was not developed, and the early Christian mind stopped short before the revolutionary doctrine that Jesus *was* God.

This fact will come as a surprise to the ordinary Christian, for we are in the habit of reading into the New Testament the interpretation of the nature of our Lord which only established itself after the best part of two centuries had elapsed since the last of its books was written. It will be well, therefore, for us to go back to the earliest documents, and to study the growth of the belief that Jesus is God.

The Epistles of St. Paul, written between 52 and 64 A.D., are our most ancient authorities; and in these Jesus is regarded as the Christos, appointed by, but quite distinct from, God the Supreme Being. "I thank my God," says St. Paul, "through Jesus Christ, for you";[1] or he speaks of "God our Father, and the Lord Jesus Christ,[2] or "the God of our Lord Jesus Christ."[3]   "To us," he writes, "there is one God the Father, of (i.e., from) whom are all things";[4] and he speaks of the prophecies "of God, concerning his Son Jesus Christ our Lord, which was made of the seed of David according to the flesh, and declared to be the Son of God according to the Spirit of holiness."[5]

The fact that St. Paul regarded Jesus Christ as the Son of God does not in itself imply, as we are

[1] Rom. i. 8.    [2] 1 Thess. i. 1.    [3] Eph. i. 17.
[4] 1 Cor. viii. 6.    [5] Rom. i. 4.

carelessly inclined to suppose, that he thought of
Him as God. The Messiah was called the Son of
God, but no Jew ever thought of him actually as
God; and even Adam could be called the Son
of God,[1] while all believers were reckoned as sons
of God.[2] It must be remembered that in the days
of the earliest Christians the idea was prevalent
that gods were in the habit of begetting sons on
earth; Perseus was the son of Zeus by a mortal
woman; Hercules was the son of Zeus by the lady
Alcmene; Plato was thought by some to be the
son of Apollo; Pythagoras was the son of a god;
Apollonius of Tyana, a contemporary of Jesus,
was the son of the god Proteus; and so forth.
This was quite a logical mental conception in
view of the fact that the gods themselves were
believed to be but aggrandised human beings:
Zeus, or Jupiter, was a big, bearded man; Apollo
was a clean-shaven youth; and even Jehovah
could walk in a garden to enjoy the cool of the
evening.[3] These old deities, though immortal,

[1] Luke iii. 38.
[2] Rom. viii. 14; and elsewhere.      [3] Gen. iii. 8.

had lived and died on earth, and hence were much like men; the tomb of Zeus was to be seen in Crete, the tombs of Dionysos and Apollo were at Delphi, the tomb of Kronos was in Sicily, that of Hermes at Hermopolis, that of Aphrodite in Cyprus, and so on. The gods were just super-men, and thus could, of course, have sons. But in pagan thought a son of "God" was not necessarily himself a deity: he was a product of "God" and thus possessed divinity, but only to a limited extent. Nevertheless, St. Paul believed that the Christos, though not God, was an eternal agent of God, who had existed before the Creation, and who "thought it not robbery to be equal with God,"[1] although not identical with Him.

In the next earliest book of the New Testament, the Book of Revelation, Jesus is still the Christ, the Son of God, but not God Himself; and in the Acts the case is the same, as we may see, for example, in the words: "Of this man's (David's) seed hath God raised a Saviour, Jesus, and through this man is preached the forgiveness of sins,"[2] or

[1] Philip. ii. 6.　　　　　　[2] Acts xiii. 23.

again: "He (God) will judge the world in righteousness by that man whom he hath ordained."[1] In the Synoptic Gospels, too, Jesus is distinct from God, and seems, indeed, definitely to repudiate the idea that He is identical with Him. Thus he says: "Why callest thou me good?—there is none good but one, that is, God";[2] and: "To sit on my right hand and on my left hand in heaven is not mine to give."[3] His cry from the cross, "My God, my God, why hast Thou forsaken me?" is not the cry of one who believed himself to be God; nor would it and these other expressions have been recorded at all if the authors of the Gospels had been attempting to place Him before the reader as indistinguishable from God.

In these Gospels He usually speaks of Himself as the "Son of Man," which, in Aramaic, is the ordinary term for a human being, but, in Hebrew, had a Messianic sound owing to its employment in the Book of Daniel,[4] and might almost be paraphrased by "The Man of Destiny." The

[1] Acts xvii. 31.    [2] Matt. xix. 17.
[3] Matt. xx. 23.    [4] Dan. vii. 13.

prophet Ezekiel was addressed by Jehovah as "Son of Man,"[1] as though this were fitting in the case of the Deity speaking to a mortal: it was, in fact, a designation implying a commission from God but negating any sort of claim to divinity. Throughout the First Century, indeed, nobody would have dreamed of regarding Jesus as God: He was the Christ, the God-sent Saviour, the Son of God, the Mediator between God and man; and in some mysterious manner He had always existed at the right hand of God, even before His incarnation. But He was not to be confused with the Supreme Being.

In the Gospel of St. John, however, written some time in the Second Century but not widely accepted at first, there is a development: Jesus is now called the *"only begotten* Son of God,"[2] a term not used elsewhere except in the First Epistle of St. John;[3] but, even so, He was still distinct from the Father. He was now the incarnate *Logos*, or "Word," which was the "divine dynamic," the

---

[1] Ez. ii. 1, and throughout.
[2] John iii. 16.                    [3] I John iv. 9.

active Agency by which God revealed Himself, yet was not understandably God Himself, though such a phrase as "the Word was with God, and the Word *was* God" could be used,[1] and Thomas could call Jesus "My Lord and my God,"[2] Jesus, too, could be supposed to say of Himself: "He that hath seen me hath seen the Father."[3] In this Gospel Jesus addresses God thus: "Thou lovedst me before the foundations of the world";[4] but the distinction is still to be observed in His words: "This is life eternal, that they might know thee, the only true God, and Jesus Christ whom thou hast sent,"[5] "I ascend to my God and to your God,"[6] and "I can of mine own self do nothing."[7]

The gradual acceptance of the *Logos* theory, which had been adopted by the author of the Gospel of St. John from the philosophy of Philo, a Hellenized Jew of Egypt, went a long way towards establishing the identification of Jesus Christ with God, and certainly carried the de-

---

[1] John i. 1–5, 14.    [2] John xx. 28.    [3] John xiv. 9.
[4] John xvii. 24.    [5] John xvii. 3.    [6] John xx. 17.
[7] John v. 30.

finition of our Lord's nature right away from that of the Christians of the First Century. Pagan thought, in fact, was now having its influence upon Christianity, and, indeed, the idea of the *Logos* itself was pagan, though it was introduced in early times into Judaism. There is considerable indication of it, I may mention, in Mithraism, Mithra being regarded as the power which upheld the sun, rather than the sun itself, an idea already appearing in the worship of Aton in Egypt in the Fourteenth Century B.C.[1]

Mithra was considered to be both begotten by, and also co-equal with Ormuzd, the Creator. Adonis, who had died and risen from the dead, was himself "God"; Attis, who also had died and risen, was in one aspect "God the Father";[2] Osiris who, again, had died and risen, was a Father-God; and so on. It was only natural, therefore, that Christianity should also identify its Founder with God; yet though the idea passes through the minds of the Christian writers of the Second and

[1] Weigall, *Life of Akhnaton*, revised ed., pp. 103, 110.
[2] Frazer, *Adonis, Attis, Osiris*, p. 174.

Third Centuries, it was widely opposed. At the beginning of the Fourth Century Lactantius,[1] a Christian " Father," stated that Jesus was Chief of the Angels, and never pretended to be God, but only God's messenger; and as late as A.D. 330 Aphraates,[2] another "Father," declares that He was not God. It was the trouble with the Arians which brought about the general adoption by the victorious Athanasians of the doctrine of Christ's godhead. The Apostles' Creed, which does not state that Jesus is God, but says: "I believe in God the Father Almighty, Maker of Heaven and earth, and in Jesus Christ His only Son," was then supplanted by the Nicene Creed: "I believe in one God the Father Almighty . . . and in one Lord Jesus Christ, begotten of His Father before all worlds, God of Gods . . . being of one substance with the Father."

This again was followed by the Athanasian Creed, of which I shall speak later, wherein the co-equal Trinity is definitely introduced for the

[1] Lactantius, *On True Wisdom*, ch. xiv.
[2] Aphraates, *Homily* xvii.

first time, and Jesus Christ is stated absolutely to be one and co-equal with God the Father. In this Creed, by the way, the famous, or, rather, infamous damnatory clauses appear, proclaiming perdition for all who do not accept its tenets: which clauses, as we have here seen, would have had the effect of consigning the apostles themselves to everlasting damnation, for all the Christians of the First Century and most of those of the Second Century would have regarded it as sheer blasphemy to say that Jesus Christ was one with God the Father, while those of the Third Century would have hesitated over such a definition, even with the support of the *Logos* theory.

In spite of these official creeds, however, the ordinary mind found a distinction between the divinity of Jesus and the Godhead of the Father; and in the Seventh Century the quite well-informed Prophet Mohammed understood Christianity to have two Gods, not one. In the Koran the Almighty is supposed to address Jesus in the words: "Hast thou said unto mankind, 'Take me as God beside God'?" and Jesus replies: "It is not for me to say that which I know to be not the truth."[1] Thus to this day the two hundred million Moslems in the world revere Jesus as "the Spirit of God," but declare, like the Unitarians, that the Godhead exists only in the Supreme Being.

The orthodox Christian of to-day, however, is compelled to believe that Jesus was the sole incarnation of an eternal personality or aspect of the Godhead which had no beginning but was always God the Son, and had always been in every way one and equal with God the Father. Personally I prefer to avoid so precise a definition, for the matter is appraised by the intuitions more easily than it is expressed in words. The teachings of the historic Jesus and the workings of His mind certainly fulfil, ethically and spiritually, our highest conception of the mind of God, and hence our Lord may be regarded in that sense as mentally divine. Moreover, if the human brain can conceive of a God at all, it must conceive of an aspect of God turned, so to speak, particularly

[1] *Koran: Sura* v.

towards mankind, which aspect may be described as the *Logos*, or divine activity; and hence the divine mind of Jesus may well be regarded as a finite and earthly manifestation of this infinite and eternally potential dynamic of Deity. But this does not exclude the appearance of that principle in other beings in this or some other planet; and all that can be said in this regard is that human history does not record any manifestation so complete as that in Jesus. Now, in the spiritual world there can be no such thing as time; and past and future must be merged into one bondless present, as is indicated in the words: "Before Abraham was, I am."[1] Therefore, not only is the *Logos* eternal, but Jesus Christ, its incarnation, is spiritually perpetual, and is as near to us now as He was to His earthly followers. He is "our Lord" in the Twentieth Century as He was in the First; but such terms as "the only begotten Son of God," "God, of the substance of the Father, and Man, of the substance of His Mother," "Who came down from Heaven," "Who sitteth

[1] John viii. 58.

at the right hand of God," and so forth, are far too crude, and too obviously borrowed from pagan thought, to be acceptable to the modern mind. His divinity, which, as we have seen, was differently defined during the first three centuries A.D., must be defined again to meet the needs of to-day's intellectuality; and the new definition must be far less categorical.

# CHAPTER XVIII

## THE TRINITY

SPIRITUAL thought must always remain outside the scope of precise investigation, and beyond the ordinary forms of expression. It is, for instance, quite useless for any man to attempt to prove by logic that there is a God; for if the matter be submitted even to the medium of words it will at once acquire a substantiality, a grossness, which it does not actually possess. And if we postulate that there is a God, the same difficulty presents itself in defining His nature. One would merely laugh if a group of aboriginal savages were to cease for a little the banging of their tomtoms in order to discuss the music of Wagner; and there is something even more ludicrous in the spectacle of a council of early Christian bishops of very limited outlook discussing the nature of Almighty God Himself—admittedly incomprehensible—and arriving at rigid conclusions to which we are still expected to adhere.

To-day, as Christians, we recognise a Trinity, that is to say, Three Persons in one God; but to the modern critical mind that definition can be no more than an expedient. God certainly is neither One Person nor Three Persons in the sense in which we are accustomed to understand the word "Person"; for He is a formless and limitless spirit. He has no position nor place in space or time; for He is Alpha and Omega, the Beginning and the End, an essence permeating all things and all times. If you suppose Him to be an enormous Force which holds the world, you will find it hard not to introduce purely material qualities into your mental conception, such as bigness and gravity—one might almost say mileage and avoirdupois. He is not a king or a ruler in any sense which we can understand, for the idea of one individual governing other individuals is a conception peculiar to human and animal life, and probably does not exist in the spiritual world. Our human senses and range of thought can in no way provide any idea of that comprehensive grasp of all things which is His. It is, indeed, derogatory to speak of the divine Being as "He" or "Him"; for there is an indication of sex in the word, and in the spiritual sphere there is no such thing.

God, in fact, as the scriptures say, is a Spirit, an omnipresent, omnipotent, omnipercipient All-in-All, completely incomprehensible to the mere reason, but in some degree intelligible to spiritual thought which has detached itself from material concepts. It is really quite vain, therefore, to exercise the mind as to whether He is Three in One, or Many in One, or simply One. He transcends numbers, eludes intellectual divisions or unifications, and rises as far above the definitions implied in Polytheism or Monotheism as infinity is above finiteness. In a spiritual sense He is Everything, He is the Whole; and therefore He can be no more than One, and no less than all the possible fractions of One. He is personal inasmuch as He pervades each one of us; and He is impersonal inasmuch as he pervades everything.

Being beyond human ideas of bulk, and outside our three-dimensional conception of position, He might as well be said to be contained in the smallest point in space as in the largest range of it; for bigness and smallness have no meaning in spiritual thought. All that the critic cares to say, in fact, is that He is timeless, formless, unlimited by space, position, size, number, or any other material consideration; and that He is at once the Whole and all the fractions, aspects, and parts of that Whole.

The idea of a co-equal Trinity, however, offers a reasonable means of expressing the inexpressible; but it must not be forgotten that Jesus Christ never mentioned such a phenomenon, and nowhere in the New Testament does the word "Trinity" appear. The idea was only adopted by the Church three hundred years after the death of our Lord; and the origin of the conception is entirely pagan.

In the Fourth Century B.C. Aristotle wrote: "All things are three, and thrice is all: and let us use this number in the worship of the gods; for, as the Pythagoreans say, everything and all things are bounded by threes, for the end, the middle, and the beginning have this number in everything, and these compose the number of the Trinity."[1]  The ancient Egyptians, whose influence on early religious thought was profound, usually arranged their gods or goddesses in trinities: there was the trinity of Osiris, Isis, and Horus, the trinity of Amen, Mut, and Khonsu, the trinity of Khnum, Satis, and Anukis, and so forth. The Hindu trinity of Brahman, Siva, and Vishnu is another of the many and widespread instances of this theological conception.

The early Christians, however, did not at first think of applying the idea to their own faith. They paid their devotions to God the Father and to Jesus Christ, the Son of God, and they recognised the mysterious and undefined existence of the Holy Spirit; but there was no thought of these three being an actual Trinity, co-equal and united in One, and the Apostles' Creed, which is the earliest of the formulated articles of Christian faith, does not mention it.

[1] Aristotle, *On the Heavens*, i.

# THE TRINITY

The application of this old pagan conception of a Trinity to Christian theology was made possible by the recognition of the Holy Spirit as the required third "Person," co-equal with the other " Persons." The idea of the Holy Spirit, as an emanation from God, had been known to the Jews from early times; but the Hebrew word which was used was *ruach*, literally meaning "wind" or "breath," this being translated into Greek as *pneuma*, which has precisely that significance, the action of the Spirit being described theologically as "pneumatic." Thus, in the Book of Genesis, where it is related that God breathed into Adam's nostrils the breath of life, the reference is to this Spirit, which had also "moved upon the face of the waters" in the earlier act of creation; and Job[1] speaks of the Spirit of God as being in his nostrils, and says: "The Spirit of God hath made me, and the breath of the Almighty hath given me life."

This conception of the Holy Spirit as the wind, or breath, of life is found in other ancient religions, and is clearly revealed in the prayer to the god

[1] Job xxvii. 3; xxxiii. 4.

Aton inscribed on the coffin of the Egyptian Pharaoh Akhnaton (1370 B.C.), which reads: "I breathe the sweet breath which comes forth from thy mouth. . . . It is my desire that I may hear thy sweet voice, the wind, that my limbs may be rejuvenated with life through love of thee. Extend to me thy hands holding thy Spirit (*Ka*), that I may receive it and may live by it."[1]

The Gospels are unanimous in attributing to Jesus various references to the Holy Spirit; but, it is only in the Gospel of St. John, which in the earliest times was not regarded as authoritative, that our Lord gives a kind of personality to this Spirit by speaking of the Comforter who is to come down to His disciples. The conception, however, was familiar to the first Christians, for St. Paul speaks of the Holy Spirit which "searcheth all things, yea, even the depths of God";[2] and he commends his readers to "the grace of the Lord Jesus Christ, the love of God, and the communion of the Holy Ghost."[3] The baptising of Christians

---

[1] Weigall, *Life of Akhnaton*, revised ed., p. 249.
[2] 1 Cor. ii. 10.    [3] 2 Cor. xiii. 14.

in the name of the Father, and of the Son, and of the Holy Ghost, seems to have been usual, too, in very early days; but the story of the coming of the Holy Spirit at the first Pentecost (the Jewish festival fifty days after the Passover) reverts to the earlier conception of the Spirit as "wind" or "breath," for it is described as arriving like "a rushing mighty wind."

Nevertheless, whether it was understood to be the divine "breath of life," or to be a personal agent of God, distinct from the *Logos*, the idea of the Spirit being co-equal with God was not generally recognised until the second half of the Fourth Century A.D. The school of Arius held the view that the Son was created by the Father and had not always been co-eternal with Him; and this led to the opposing party not only emphasising the equality of the Father and Son (just as Mithra in the great rival religion, Mithraism, was both son of Ormuzd, the Creator, and at the same time co-equal with him), but also emphasising the co-equality of the Holy Spirit with the Father and the Son.

In the year 381 the Council of Constantinople added to the earlier Nicene Creed a description of the Holy Spirit as "the Lord, and giver of life, who proceedeth from the Father, who with the Father and Son together is worshipped and glorified." But the great opponent of the Arians was Athanasius, Bishop of Alexandria in Egypt; and, as has been said above, the Egyptian religion, which had not yet died out, was permeated with the idea of trinities. Thus, the Athanasian creed, which is a later composition but reflects the general conceptions of Athanasius and his school, formulated the conception of a co-equal Trinity wherein the Holy Spirit was the third "Person"; and so it was made a dogma of the faith, and belief in the Three in One and One in Three became a paramount doctrine of Christianity, though not without terrible riots and bloodshed.

Now, in the Constantinople creed the Holy Spirit was said to proceed from the Father, but at the Synod of Toledo in 589 the famous *filioque* was added, making the sentence read: "who proceedeth from the Father *and the Son*," as the

Church of England has it in the Communion Service in the Prayer Book to-day. But this raised a furious storm, and became one of the chief reasons of the break between the Churches of the West and East, the latter believing that the Spirit emanated from the Father only.

The modern mind has outgrown this splitting of hairs; and as the conception of divinity expands and develops, the desire to define the godhead fades. To-day a Christian thinker recognises the three aspects of divinity—the Father, the Son or *Logos*, and the Holy Spirit, and finds no cause to repudiate the idea of such a Trinity; but at the same time he has no wish to be precise about it, more especially since the definition is obviously pagan in origin and was not adopted by the Church until nearly three hundred years after Christ.

# CHAPTER XIX

### THE JESUS OF HISTORY

IN the previous chapters an attempt has been made
to disentangle the historical figure of Jesus from
the web of theological speculation and legendary
tales which has grown up around Him; for Protes-
tantism should be more than "a return to primitive Christianity," as it is sometimes defined: it
should be a return to the Jesus of history. Let us
pause, therefore, and ask ourselves how much that
is really historical we know about our Lord's
character, and what is the basis of our belief in
Him.

In the first place, what is the documentary
evidence? There is only one document in existence which can claim to have been written by a
man who actually knew Jesus, namely, the First
Epistle General of Peter. The evidence that this
letter was written by Peter himself is pretty con-

clusive. Anybody who reads this tragic Epistle will see at once that it was composed at a time when the persecution of the scattered little band of Christians was beginning to take place; and the author implores his readers not to be frightened, or to think that the new odium in which they were held was something strange and horrible which had come upon them,[1] but to realise that, like Jesus Himself, they may be called upon to suffer for the truth. Now Mommsen and others have held that the persecution of the Christians began in the time of Nero (A.D. 54–68), particularly after the great fire in Rome in A.D. 64, though the statements of Tacitus are sometimes questioned.[2] Tertullian, indeed, definitely records the early tradition that Peter was martyred under Nero. Certain critics, such as Holtzmann and Weizsäcker, it is true, have attempted to show that these persecutions were not serious until after A.D. 100, and that therefore this Epistle may belong to that date, and hence may not have been written by Peter; but certainly as early as the time

[1] I Pet. iv. 12.　　　　[2] Tacitus, *Ann.*, xv. 44.

of Irenæus (A.D. 180), Peter was believed to have been its author, and no critic has denied that this authorship is possible, while the overwhelming opinion, from the internal evidence, is that the document is really from the actual pen of Peter or his secretary, and was written shortly before his martyrdom, probably in A.D. 64.

Peter, then, the only author who knew Jesus personally, describes Him as One Who "suffered for us, leaving us an example . . . : who did no sin, neither was guile found in his mouth: who, when he was reviled, reviled not again; when he suffered, he threatened not, but committed himself to Him that judgeth righteously: who his own self bare our sins in his own body on the tree . . . : by whose stripes we are healed."[1]   He says that he himself was a witness of these sufferings,[2] though his readers in Pontus, Galatia, Cappadocia, Bithynia, and elsewhere, had not actually seen Jesus, as he had.[3]   He tells how He was put to death in the flesh, but was brought back to life,[4] and how He had gone to heaven,[5] but would very

---

[1] I Pet. ii. 21–24.    [2] v. I.    [3] i. 8.    [4] iii. 18.    [5] iii. 22.

shortly return.[1]  In order to follow the example of Jesus, he urges his readers to love one another, to be compassionate, pitiful, courteous; not rendering evil for evil, but meeting insults with blessings; to be charitable, hospitable, humble; to do good, eschew evil, and to seek peace; to abstain from the lusts of the flesh, to avoid malice, envy, and evil speaking; to submit to authority, to fear God and honour the King; to accept blows and reproaches for righteousness' sake; and above all, to receive the Faith like little children, trusting in God's mercy.

This is the earliest revelation of the surpassingly beautiful character of Jesus that we possess, and also the earliest evidence of His historicity, written, almost without doubt, by one who had known Him.  St. Paul's Epistles come next in historic importance, for though Paul had not actually been with Jesus during His ministry, he had learnt about Him from those who had.[2]  The Epistles which are unquestionably from the hand of Paul, and which were written about twenty to

---

[1] I Pet. iv. 7.                    [2] I Cor. xv. 3.

thirty years after the Crucifixion, are those to the Romans, Galatians, and Corinthians; other Epistles are most probably to be dated to this early period, but since it is just possible that they were written by later hands, they must not be cited here.

Now Paul, like Peter, speaks of Jesus, in these unquestioned documents, as being about to return in glory to judge mankind;[1] but this fervent belief that the Second Coming was imminent shows clearly that the departure of Jesus must have been recent, and must have been to him an established fact. Moreover, he is able to say that he knew Peter and had met James, the brother of Jesus;[2] he can speak of other persons being still alive who had seen Him;[3] he can speak of His parentage;[4] he can write of the Last Supper as a real event;[5] and the story of the Crucifixion[6] and of the return from the dead is the basis of his faith.[7] Yet he was writing at a time so near to that at which these

---

[1] Rom. xiii. 12; I Cor. i. 7; iv. 5; vii. 29.     [2] Gal. i. 18, 19.
[3] I Cor. xv. 6.     [4] Rom. i. 3.
[5] I Cor. xi. 23.     [6] I Cor. ii. 2.
[7] Rom. vi. 4; I Cor. xv. 4.

events were said to have occurred that it is impossible to suppose him to have been completely deceived in regard to their actuality. He must have known, too, much of the life and teaching of Jesus, for he states that he has His instructions on one matter but not on another,[1] and says: "Be ye imitators of me, even as I am of Christ."[2]

He speaks of the meekness and gentleness of Jesus, and of His simplicity; and says that He was rich yet for our sakes became poor; and that He did not please Himself. Following the teachings of our Lord, he preaches charity, love, joy, peace, long-suffering, gentleness, goodness, meekness, temperance, and faith. He says that the law must be studied in newness of spirit, and not according to the letter, and that it is all contained in the one phrase: "Thou shalt love thy neighbour as thyself." He tells his readers to love one another, to be patient, to condescend to men of low estate, to live amicably, to overcome evil with good; and he urges them to be law-abiding and to give due respect to the authorities.

[1] 1 Cor. vii. 6, 25.   [2] 1 Cor. xi. 1.

Thus, from these early Epistles we obtain sufficient evidence not only to establish the historicity of Jesus, but also to reveal to some extent His character. The beauty of His life was such that Peter, who knew Him, and Paul, who knew His brother, could deem Him a man without sin, one who to them was obviously the Son of God. I cannot recall in history a well-authenticated instance, like this, of a leader inspiring his immediate followers with such utter adoration.

Such, then, is the Jesus revealed by these first documents; but besides the Epistles we have the Synoptic Gospels, wherein a clear basis of fact is to be observed under the legendary matter. The character of Jesus as it appears in these books is to be relied on as authentic, on the whole, because, as I have explained in an earlier chapter, Bishop Papias, writing about A.D. 140, tells us that Matthew made a collection of the sayings of our Lord, which was pretty certainly used in the composition of the Gospels, and that Mark, Peter's pupil, collected notes of His sayings and acts, which were similarly used; and the full picture of Him created in the mind by the Gospels corresponds exactly to the outline derived from the earlier Epistles. When the incredible events are deleted from the story, we discover a figure which by no stretch of the imagination can we regard as mythical: a figure which, nearly two thousand years later, still stands as the ideal of the perfect man whom the modern mind can accept as guide, master, and Lord.

What do we know of His actual life? We know nothing of his youth that can be called authentic: He comes before us only at His baptism by John, in the year A.D. 28 or 29, when, as the son of the village carpenter, He leaves His home to preach the Kingdom of Heaven, retiring first, for a short period of unknown length, into the wilderness to meditate and pray. Collecting a few disciples, He begins His wandering ministry, healing the sick by His exceptional powers so that soon all manner of wild stories are told of Him in this regard, and His fame spreads far and wide. Everywhere He electrifies His hearers, and the rumour circulates that a great prophet has come out of Galilee, with the result that a concerted opposition begins to appear amongst those to whom His views are inimical.  On more than one occasion He is in danger of being stoned to death, but nothing daunts His gallant spirit.

Gradually he becomes conscious that He is the Messiah, and for one brief moment it seems as though He were about to raise the whole country. He enters Jerusalem surrounded by an excited mob; but the demonstration, to which He was never a party, is a complete failure, and at nightfall He leaves the city.  Next day He enters it again, and there is more commotion; but now the authorities are aroused, and arrangements are made for His arrest.  Two days before the Passover, probably April 6th, in the year A.D. 30, He eats His last meal with His disciples; but now He knows that death awaits Him unless He take to flight.  Yet, rather than abandon His mission, He decides to be faithful to the truth that is in Him, even though it lead Him to the grave.  He knows now that His kingdom, the kingdom of the Messiah, is not of this world.

That night He is arrested, and next morning He is tried. The execution of a criminal in the guise of the annual *Bar Abbas* is about to take place; but the mob frantically urges the authorities to crucify Jesus in place of the chosen victim, and thus He is made to play the part of this yearly Paschal "sacrifice." The immemorial rites are performed: He is scourged, dressed in royal robes, mocked, and "hung up before the Lord" on the traditional tree or cross; but before nightfall a condition indistinguishable from death descends upon Him as by a miracle, and His sufferings, which had wrung no angry protest from His lips, are at an end. His friends take Him down from the cross, and lay Him in a tomb, intending to bury Him at daybreak after the Passover; but before that hour has arrived He has come back to life. He tries to tell His disciples that He is alive, but they will not believe Him; He goes back to Galilee, and there talks to them; but in their eyes He is a spirit risen from the dead. At last He leaves them, saying that He will return; but He never comes back, and that is the end of the historic story.

It is the story of a sublime character heroically facing death for His principles, impelled forward by the knowledge revealed to Him in His study of the Prophets, that even so the Messiah must suffer for the good of the world. Afterwards in thinking over these events, His disciples could not recall a single fault in Him: He was the perfect man, and as such He is described in the earliest documents we possess, as well as in the later Gospels and other books. His actions are marked by complete unselfishness and supreme heroism; His power is demonstrated in His many healings of the sick, and in the undying adoration which He aroused; and the perfection of His thought is displayed in His recorded sayings and teachings which, though they have many isolated parallels in the best of the world's wisdom, have never been equalled in the mass as the product of one brain.

# CHAPTER XX

THE outstanding characteristic of the teaching of Jesus was its simplicity. He reduced religion almost to two principles—the love of God and the brotherhood of man; and often He said that the whole doctrine was capable of being understood by a child, and, indeed, that it was necessary to its understanding that the novice should become a child again, which means to say that he should recover that clear gaze of childhood which was his before his mental vision became veiled by the perplexities of accepted sacerdotalism. The entire theology of Jesus may be summed up in four sentences: That God was the loving Father of mankind, in whose sight all men were equal; that He poured out His goodness through the Holy Spirit; that He had promised to send a Delegate,

215

or "Anointed-one," to lead the nations to Him and establish the Kingdom of Heaven on earth; and that the reward of goodness and brotherly love was eternal life, but the penalty of evil annihilation.

In our Lord's fight for simple faith against the crushing complexities of religious tradition, He vigorously denounced the rigid formalities and ceremonies of Judaism, and deliberately broke its laws. He refused to observe the Sabbath;[1] He appalled the orthodox by saying that it was not necessary to perform the ceremonial washing of the hands before eating;[2] He denounced showy prayers;[3] He consorted with publicans (i.e., tax-gatherers) against whom there was a sort of religious taboo;[4] He did not keep the fasts with any punctiliousness;[5] He said: "Let the dead bury their dead,"[6] by which He meant that the usual prolonged ritual of conventional mourning in connection with a public funeral was an exercise

---

[1] Mark ii. 23–28.
[2] Mark vii. 2–8.
[3] Matt. vi. 5.
[4] Mark ii. 16.
[5] Mark ii. 18.
[6] Matt. viii. 22.

only for the mentally defunct; and, in general, He taught that as new wine could not be put into old bottles,[1] so His new doctrine could not be cramped into the old conventions.

It is a matter for earnest reflection that these teachings of Jesus, which were so vehemently directed against the formalities of religion, were themselves resolved into a formal religion, and that a few centuries after His ministry Christianity had developed into a highly complex, ritualistic, and conventional faith. But such is the fate of most religious reformations, from that of Buddha to that of Mrs. Eddy: each reformer attacks the empty conventions and complications of the existing church, propounds a simple doctrine free from religious formality, and, after a few years, becomes the ceremonially revered founder of an equally formal and intricate religion. Jesus did not attempt to establish a Church at all, for those words in which such an institution is implied seem to be later inventions or interpolations, as, for example: "Upon this rock I will build my

[1] Mark ii. 22.

church."[1] Yet within a few decades Christianity had developed a complex theology altogether beyond the grasp of the specified child; and within a few centuries it had become a ritualistic religion dangerously prone to the empty formalities its Founder had denounced. When the thoughtful layman contemplates the simple figure of Jesus, the teacher of unadulterated truths, and then turns his attention to the ceremonial chanting of the Athanasian Creed, he can hardly fail to be conscious of a kind of dismay; and it must occur to him that since a Christian can best be at one with Christ by interesting himself in those things which interested Him, and since the thing that emphatically did *not* interest Him was ecclesiastical doctrine and ritual, there can be little spiritual benefit to be derived from participation in the priestly rite.

Some sort of organised religion, however, is necessary, and some kind of formal worship is required, if only to check the exuberance of the individual; and, provided that its dogmas and its

[1] Matt. vi. 18. See pages 137-138.

ritual can be kept as simple and as natural as possible, a formalised Church cannot be far from the approval of our Lord. But it should never be forgotten that sacerdotalism, priestcraft, forms and ceremonies, and all the elaborate staging of public worship, excited Jesus to the chief outbursts of indignation of which there is any seemingly authentic record in His ministry. He came to teach men how to lead a man's life, how to follow the guiding light of the divine flame which burns in every human heart, without dread of the consequences, without fear of the opposition of convention or tradition or custom. His influence is that of the everlasting rebel against the Phariseeism of society. He preached the most simple faith which has ever been propounded; but let us see what the Church, founded in His name, made of it.

His earliest followers read into the story of His Crucifixion all the complicated Judaic beliefs in regard to the shedding of blood for the remission of sins, and made of Him the immemorial Paschal sacrifice, tortured to appease the wrath of God.

The Pagan converts added to this interpretation their ancient traditions in regard to the sacramental sufferings, death, and resurrection of Adonis, Hyacinth, Attis, Osiris, Mithra, and all the other gods who had died for the sins of mankind; and, finding the new faith deficient in regard to the feminine element in divinity, they began to raise the mother of Jesus to the position left vacant in their hearts by the rejection of Isis, Cybele, Demeter, Diana of the Ephesians, and the other great maternal goddesses. For their sacraments they took the old Judaic baptism by water, and added thereto the mysteries of the Mithraic rite; and from the worship of Mithra, too, they took the communion of the Bread and the Cup with all its long lineage from the forgotten ceremonies of cannibalism.

Thus and thus they presented thenselves to the pagan world, in the name of Christ, as one of the most complex of the pagan faiths; and after suffering persecution under Nero in A.D. 64, under Marcus Aurelius in A.D. 166 and 177, under Decius in A.D. 250 and 251, and under Diocletian in A.D.

303, as the followers of "an odious superstition,"[1] they were at last granted toleration by Galerius in A.D. 311. Constantine was baptised into their faith on his death-bed in A.D. 337, but Julian, who reigned from A.D. 361 to 363, rounded upon them for the persecutions which they, in their turn, were now inflicting upon the other faiths. Their power, however, was by this time too tremendous to be overthrown, and in A.D. 391 Theodosius the Great established Christianity as the sole religion of the State.

The Christian doctrine had now defined itself, not without riot and bloodshed, along the lines of that extraordinary composition still, unfortunately, having a place in the Anglican Prayer Book, namely, the Athanasian Creed, traditionally attributed to Bishop Athanasius of Alexandria, in Egypt, A.D. 293-373, but, although exactly wording his views, more probably a European work of the Fifth Century. In this creed the faith is seen to have developed into the recognition of three Persons in One God, the first of these Persons being

[1] Pliny, *Letter* xcviii.

God the Father, once implacably hostile to man, but reconciled by the vicarious human-sacrifice of the second Person, God the Son, and the Third Person being God the Holy Ghost. Belief in this Trinity, the idea of which was borrowed mainly from pagan Egypt, was made the *sine quâ non* of salvation, and the Creed stated that those who did not adhere to it should perish everlastingly—words belonging to the dark ages and not fit for modern presentation. By the first half of the Fifth Century the obscure and unassuming Mary had become the great Queen of Heaven, so that the Prophet Mohammed in the Seventh Century could suppose that the Christians were polytheists, having, besides God, a Goddess Mary and her Son, yet another God.[1]

From Pagan mythology Christianity had unconsciously taken over many a wonderful story and had incorporated it into the life of Jesus: from Mithraism the tale of the birth in the cave and the adoration of the shepherds; from Adonis-worship the tale of the Star in the East; from

[1] *Koran: Sura* v. 116.

Dionysos-worship the tale of the turning of water into wine; and so forth. From Mithraism had come the use of bell, candle, and holy water;[1] the employment of catacombs; the selection of the Vatican Mount as the sacred site; and many another usage. The idea of being washed in the blood of the lamb came from Mithraism and other pagan faiths; and being "born again" is an expression borrowed from these and from Isis-worship, there being a record of a man who was initiated into the Isis mysteries, and so "born again."[2]

In the liturgy and ritual gradually built up by the new State Church, pagan influence reveals itself in the ceremonious court paid to God, which is entirely un-Christian in principle. Never once, so far as we know, had Jesus spoken of or addressed God as a mighty King, never once had He named Him "Almighty"; for, although He acknowledged it, He had usually refrained from referring to the Father's omnipotence and majesty. The ending

---

[1] *Encyc. Brit.*, 11th ed., vol. xvii., p. 624.

[2] Apuleius, *Metamorphoses*, xi. 16.

223

of the Lord's Prayer—"For thine is the Kingdom, the power, and the glory"—is only given in the Gospel of St. Luke, and is undoubtedly a later addition to the text. It was God's love, not His kingly puissance, which Jesus wished to stress; but paganism regarded its gods as potentates, and the Church followed its example, its ritual being based upon the ancient tradition of behaviour in the presence of an earthly King, and the priests approaching the throne of God with flattery upon their lips. "High and mighty King of Kings," He is still called in the Anglican Prayer Book, "Lord of Lords, the only Ruler of Princes," "Sovereign Commander of all the world." "We magnify Thy glorious name," "we glorify Thee, we give thanks to Thee for Thy great glory," "O most mighty God": in this manner the clergy to this day endeavour to propitiate with their blandishments a God who in their hearts they must know to be infinitely above this sort of thing.

Step by step the ritual was elaborated, and between the Sixth and Ninth Centuries the simple clothes of the clergy developed into rich and royal vestments. The amice and the alb, the cincture and the tunicle, the dalmatic and the stole, the chasuble and the maniple, came into fashion; and in the Ninth Century the Pontifical gloves made their appearance. In the Tenth Century the mitre of the bishops arrived; and the Eleventh Century saw the coming of special shoes and stockings for the dignitaries of the Church. At the Reformation these things were discarded by the Anglican Church, only the surplice and the square cap being allowed; but in the Nineteenth Century vestments came back into use, and though they were pronounced illegal in 1870, the objection to them has gradually been over-ridden in England, until to-day the Anglo-Catholic party adorn themselves, as do the Roman Catholics and others, in finery indeed wonderful to behold. These vestments are pleasing to the eye, and historically have great interest; but their history does not carry us back, specifically, further than the Dark Ages, though the dressing-up habit, especially in reference to divine worship, may be traced to the Stone Age. I suppose there is no critic who would have the hardihood to say that Jesus did not set His face against all that sort of display; and yet . . . well, it is dramatic, and the dramatic instinct is too hopelessly confused with the religious ever to be disentangled except by really spiritual natures.

Meanwhile many of the old heathen gods had been taken into the Church as saints. Castor and Pollux became St. Cosmo and St. Damien; Dionysos, many of whose attributes were attached to St. John the Baptist, still holds his place as St. Denis of Paris; Diana Illythia is now St. Yllis of Dôle; the Dia Victoria is worshipped in the Basses Alpes as St. Victoire; and so forth. All over Christendom, pagan sacred places were perpetuated by the erection of Christian chapels or churches on the same sites; and there are hundreds of shrines dedicated to the Madonna on ground once sacred to nymphs or goddesses, while the holy wells or springs of heathendom are now the holy wells of the Church. The statues of Jupiter and Apollo became those of St. Peter and St. Paul; and the figures of Isis were turned into those of the Virgin Mary, while the Madonna-lilies are none other than the ancient sacred lotus-flowers of Isis and Astarte. And by the score old heathen customs were given Christian sanction, as, for example, in the case of that of eating fish on Friday, Friday being the day dedicated in many religions to the Mother-goddesses who were the patrons of the fisheries; or as in the case of the continued celebration of pagan festivals, of which I shall speak in the next chapters.

Such, then, is the theology, and such the Church, which has grown up in the name of the carpenter's son, who had confided His simple truths to a few ragged fishermen and peasants. Christianity is very largely a pagan faith; yet behind its pomp and vanities, beneath its preposterous complexities, there is still to be found the Jesus of history, and in His teaching and example is the world's salvation. If only we can get back to Him. . . .

# CHAPTER XXI

## SUNDAY OBSERVANCE

IN the early Christian Church there were no festivals, holy days, or Sabbaths, for, as Chrysostom says, "the whole of time is a festival unto Christians, because of the excellency of the good things which have been given"; or, as Origen puts it, "to the perfect Christian all his days are the Lord's."[1] Socrates, the ecclesiastical historian, also tells us that "the apostles had no thought of appointing festival days, but only of promoting a life of blamelessness and piety." When the Church had become a State institution, however, the need of holy days and festivals began to be felt, and, indeed, it was essential to give a Christian significance to those of pagan origin which could not be suppressed. The clergy, for example, could not prevent the people in various countries

[1] Origen, *Cont. Cels.*, viii. 22.

celebrating a great holiday at Easter in honour of the resurrection of Attis and other gods; and they were obliged, therefore, to consent to perpetuate this old custom, as Socrates tells us, by giving it a Christian interpretation. Socrates remarks, too, that many other pagan customs had been established in the Church in like manner; and Bede has preserved a letter written by Pope Gregory in the year 601, wherein he states that the policy of the Church is to adapt these old pagan holy days to Christian ideas, and not to suppress them.[1]

The Church, in fact, was quite frank in regard to its appropriations; but time has spread its veil over these matters, and now it will come as a disconcerting surprise to many Christians to learn that the festivals which we call Christmas and Easter are pagan, not Christian, in origin, and that the same is to be said of other great Church feasts, such as that of the Assumption, that of St. John the Baptist, that of St. George, and so on, while the fast of Lent is also pagan. I have already mentioned that Sunday, too, was a pagan

[1] Bede, *Eccles. Hist.*, ch. xxx.

holy day; and in this chapter I propose to discuss the origin of this custom of keeping one day in the week as a Sabbath, or "day of rest," and to show that the practice was forcefully opposed by Jesus Christ.

The origin of the seven-day week, which was used by the Jews and certain other peoples, but not till later by the Greeks or Romans, is to be sought in some primitive worship of the moon, for the custom of keeping the day of the new moon and that of the full moon as festivals, which is widely found in antiquity, implies the recognition of a cycle of about 14 days, of which a week of 7 days is the half, the actual length of a week thus determined being 7⅜ days. Now the Babylonians had early adopted the seven-day week, and their calendars contain directions for the abstention from certain secular acts on stated days which seem to correspond to seventh days, and were called "Sabbaths"; and though the Jewish Sabbath cannot be directly traced to Babylonian usage, the institution is obviously derived from moon-worship and from the concomitant recognition of the number seven as calendrically sacred. The Jews attributed the holiness of the seventh day to the fact that God was supposed to have rested from His six-days' creative labours on that day; but this was itself a legend derived from Babylonian mythology, and was not the original reason why the seventh day was a day of rest.

It happened that there were seven "planets" known to ancient astronomy—the sun, the moon, Mars, Mercury, Jupiter, Venus, and Saturn; and where a seven-day week was in use there is reason to suppose that the days were dedicated to these planets. The first day of the week was dedicated to the sun, which was the most important of the celestial bodies, and the last day of the week, the seventh day, was dedicated to Saturn, which was the planet most distant from the sun. But this planet was identified in ancient Eastern religion with a god of ill-omen, and hence the seventh day gradually became in primitive times an unlucky day, upon which no work could be successfully undertaken. For this reason it passed at length into a day of rest, and, later, the legend of the creation was adapted so as to explain the fact.

The Israelites developed the idea of this seventh day being one of rest, and already in the time of Moses the laws on the subject were so strict that a man was put to death for gathering firewood on the Sabbath,[1] and even the lighting of a fire was forbidden on that day under penalty of death[2]— to such lengths of folly can superstition carry the human mind. In the time of our Lord the orthodox Jews kept the Sabbath not much less strictly; but Jesus very definitely opposed Himself to this observance, and, according to the Gospel of St. John,[3] actually risked His life in attempting to emancipate His followers from the bondage of the custom by deliberately breaking the Sabbath laws. There must, indeed, have been a tremendously strong and clear tradition amongst early Christians that Jesus had freed them entirely from Sabbath observance, for in the Gospels He is reported as omitting the Fourth Commandment—"Keep holy the Sabbath-day"—from His

[1] Num. xv. 35.    [2] Ex. xxxv. 2, 3.    [3] John v. 18.

list[1] of ordinances; while St. Paul also omits it,[2] and attacks the Galatians for observing any special day as holy,[3] his attitude being confirmed in the Epistle to the Colossians, where it is said that neither the Sabbath nor any other day should be observed as sacred.[4] Irenæus, one of the Christian Fathers of the Second Century, says definitely[5] that Jesus cancelled the observance of the Sabbath; Tertullian, in the Third Century, writes[6] that "to Christians Sabbaths are unknown"; Victorinus, in the Fourth Century, repeats that Jesus abolished "any Sabbath observance"[7]; and Justin, Clement, Origen, Eusebius, Epiphanius, Cyril, Jerome, and other "Fathers" all say the same thing in the most emphatic terms.

But while the Saturday Sabbath of the Jews was thus abolished by the early Christians, and no other day was allowed to take its place as a Sabbath, it became the custom already, in the First Century, to regard Sunday, the first day of

---

[1] Matt. xix. 18–19; Mark x. 19.
[2] Rom. xiii. 9.  [3] Gal. iv. 9–11.  [4] Col. ii. 16.
[5] Irenæus, *Against Heresies*.  [6] Tertullian, *Ans. to Jews*.
[7] Victorinus, *Ante Nicene*, bk. xviii.

the week, as a day specially appropriate for the meetings of the faithful, ostensibly because Jesus had risen from the dead on that day. Thus we read[1] that the early disciples in Troas met weekly on Sundays for exhortation and breaking of bread; and in the *Didache, or Teaching of the Apostles,*[2] Christians are told to come together on "the Lord's Day," and we know from Justin Martyr and Tertullian that the term "Lord's Day" meant Sunday, the day of the Lord's resurrection. Tertullian is emphatic that any special worship on the Lord's Day is unlawful[3]; but Ignatius says that Christians do observe that day,[4] and Dionysius of Corinth speaks of it as holy,[5] while both Irenæus and Tertullian go so far as to say that it ought to be regarded as a day on which the faithful should rest from their usual labours. Pliny, writing in 112 A.D., says that Christians were wont to meet before dawn and sing a hymn on a certain day of the week—by which undoubtedly

---

[1] Acts xx. 7.
[2] *Didache*, ch. xiv.
[3] Tertullian, *De Corona.*
[4] Ignatius, *Ad. Magn.*, ix.
[5] Dionysius, quoted by Eusebius, *Hist. Ecc.*, iv. 23.

he means Sunday—and later on to eat a communal meal together.[1]

In general, therefore, the evidence is that the earliest Christians absolutely refused to observe any Sabbath at all, but that gradually Sunday came to be recognised as the weekly meeting-day, and later, to some extent, as a day of rest, though any suggestion that it was a real substitute for the old Sabbath, or that it was to be observed with corresponding strictness, was hotly repudiated. Now Sunday, being dedicated to the sun, had been for long the holy day in the solar religions of paganism, and it was the day specially revered by the worshippers of Mithra,[2] being probably called by them also "the Lord's Day." Thus the fact that Jesus had left the tomb on Sunday does not seem to have been the real reason why that day was particularly reverenced by the early Christians, for they might have been expected to have selected Friday as the weekly day of quiet commemoration, that being the day of His death.

[1] Pliny, *Letter* xcviii.
[2] J. M. Robertson, *Pagan Christs*, p. 429.

It seems more likely, in fact, that they were influenced here, as in so many other matters, by pagan custom, and that Sunday came to be celebrated because the Mithraists and other sun-worshippers regarded it as a sacred holiday, and the habit could not be suppressed.

In the year 321 the Emperor Constantine, who was not yet a declared Christian, but was still hovering between paganism and Christianity, issued a decree making Sunday a compulsory day of rest; but the fact that he speaks of Sunday as "the venerable day of the Sun" shows that he was thinking of it as a traditional sun-festival at the same time that he thought of it as a Christian holy-day. This decree, however, was not popular, and finally it was repealed by the Emperor Leo in the Ninth Century. But, in the West, Charlemagne forbade work of any sort on Sundays; and in England the laws of the Anglo-Saxon Kings, Ina, Athelstan, and Æthelred, prohibited marketing and certain kinds of labour or sport on that day. Later on, however, Sunday came to be observed throughout Europe as it is still observed by Roman Catholics, namely, as a day on which, like our Christmas, people went to church in the morning and then gave themselves over to rest or to holiday-making and sports. This is undoubtedly the nearest approximation to the early Christian method of observing Sunday.

At the Reformation Luther was emphatic in his denunciation of those who kept Sunday as particularly holy, and he advised his followers to dance or feast on that day in order to oppose its sacred observance.[1] Zwingli, the Swiss reformer, said: "It is lawful on the Lord's Day after divine service for any man to pursue his labours"; and even John Knox, in referring to the Sabbath, said that "Christians should have nothing to do with the superstitious observance of days." The Puritans of the Seventeenth Century in England, however, reverted to the old Jewish idea which Jesus had opposed; and this so angered King James I that he issued a *Book of Sports* for Sundays, urging his subjects to play games on that day. But after that time various legal enactments were passed

[1] Luther, in *Table Talk*.

under Puritanical influence; and public opinion became so far estranged from the authentic teaching of Jesus Christ that it supported the strictest observance of Sunday as the Sabbath.

To-day, however, people are beginning again to make holiday on Sundays; and though they are doing so without asking the permission of their religious pastors, they might, if they were to go into the matter, give them chapter and verse in support of their position, and might defy the Biblical student to provide one single word in Scripture to justify Christianity's approval of the Commandment of Moses, "Remember to keep holy the Sabbath-day," or its resuscitation from the limbo into which our Lord so definitely consigned it. The refusal of certain people to work or to play on Sundays owing to religious scruples is evidence of so un-Christian and so gross a superstition that the mind of the thinking man is staggered by it; and it is astounding to find that the Mosaic Commandment to refrain from all work on that day is still solemnly read by the ministers of that same Jesus Christ who dared all to abolish it.

# CHAPTER XXII

## THE ORIGIN OF THE EPIPHANY

THE date of the birthday of our Lord is unknown.
Birthdays in the East usually go uncelebrated, for
parents, unless they be very highly placed, seldom
remember the exact days on which their children
were born; and, indeed, even the approximate
age of an Oriental is often forgotten. There is no
evidence that Jesus knew on what day He had
been born, and certainly His disciples did not
know: even His mother seems to have forgotten,
for although she lived with the disciples after
the Crucifixion,[1] she evidently was unable to give
them a date on which to commemorate the event,
and our present Christmas, December 25th, as I
shall explain in the next chapter, was never
thought by the Church to be the real date. Nor
did custom inspire the disciples with any desire

[1] Acts i. 14.

to make an anniversary of the Nativity at all; and, in fact, Origen, writing in about the year 245, says that it is most improper to keep the birthday of Jesus Christ, as though He were a mere king or Pharaoh. The general feeling in early times was that His divine life commenced only at His baptism by John in the sacred waters of the Jordan; but here, again, the date was unknown, and when, in the Second Century, Christians began to desire to commemorate His baptism, they had to consider what date should be chosen for the anniversary. Finally they selected, in part deliberately and in part under the influence of ancient custom, the date January 6th because this was the day on which the sacred waters were blessed both in the religion of Osiris and in that of Dionysos.

I have already shown that the worship of Osiris must have made its influence felt upon the early Christian mind, for his death and resurrection were widely celebrated; but we must now consider the influence of the worship of Dionysos, who was identified by the Greeks with Osiris.

# THE ORIGIN OF THE EPIPHANY

Dionysos, whose father, as in the Christian story, was "God" but whose mother was a mortal woman,[1] was represented in the East as a bearded young man of dignified appearance, who had not only taught mankind the use of the vine, but had also been a law-giver, promoting the arts of civilisation, preaching happiness, and encouraging peace. He, like Jesus, had suffered a violent death, and had descended into hell, but his resurrection and ascension had followed; and these were commemorated in his sacred rites. According to one legend he had turned himself into a bull, and in this guise had been cut to pieces by his enemies; and according to another legend he had been transformed into a ram. His worshippers were wont to tear a bull or a goat to pieces and to devour the meat raw, thereby eating the flesh and drinking the blood of their god in a frenzied eucharist. Various animals were sacred to him, amongst which were the ram and the ass; and in regard to the latter there was a story that he had once ridden upon two asses and had afterwards

[1] Lucian, *Dialogi Deorum*, ix. 2.

caused them to become celestial constellations, in which legend we may perhaps see him as a solar god and may connect him with the zodiacal sign Cancer which, in the Babylonian zodiac, was the Ass and Foal, and which marked the zenith of the sun's power and the beginning of its decline towards winter.

Now the ministry of Jesus culminated in His entry into Jerusalem, after which the events led quickly downwards to the tomb; and on that occasion He is described as riding, like Dionysos, upon two asses, that is to say, upon "an ass and a colt, the foal of an ass,"[1] which suggests that the second ass may have been added to the story under the influence of astrological lore. The Gnostics undoubtedly identified Jesus with this sign, for a Gnostic gem has been found, whereon an ass and its foal are shown together with the crab (Cancer), and an abbreviated Latin inscription gives the words: "Our Lord Jesus Christ, the Son of God."[2] It is a recognised law of

[1] Matt. xxi. 5, 7.
[2] J. M. Robertson, *Christianity and Mythology*, p. 369.

mythology that a god is identical with the species of animal sacred to him; and just as Dionysos is thus, in one of his aspects, an ass, so Jesus, who had become confused with Dionysos in ignorant pagan minds, seems to have been identified with that animal, for a drawing has been found upon a wall of the Domus Gelotiana on the Palatine,[1] in which He is shown hanging on the cross but having the head of an ass. The ass, again, is associated with the vine, the chief symbol of Dionysos, for Justin Martyr[2] speaks of the ass as tied to a vine; and Jesus, again, is identified with the vine both in the words of the Gospel of St. John, "I am the true vine,"[3] which, to pagan ears, was tantamount to saying "I am Dionysos," and in the *Didache*, where the contents of the Eucharistic cup are described as "the holy vine of David,"[4] which means not only that the wine was regarded symbolically as the blood of Jesus, but that Jesus was regarded symbolically as Wine.

[1] Now in the Kircherian Museum of the Collegio Romano; see F. Kraus, *Das Spottcrucifix.*

[2] Justin Martyr, *Apol.*, i, 32.

[3] John xv. 1.

[4] *Didache*, ix.

The great festival of Dionysos was widely celebrated on January 6th. But Dionysos, as has been said, was identified with the Egyptian god Osiris, and in Egypt there seems to have been an ancient Nile-festival at the same time of year, which the Christian Copts celebrate to this day as the *Îd el-Ghitâs*, or "Festival of the Immersion," whereat the river is blessed, and holy water is poured into it, after which the people plunge into the stream. The date of this festival is the 11th day of the month Tobi, which in ancient times corresponded to January 6th. But the god Osiris was, in one of his aspects, the deity of the Nile;[1] and thus this Nile-festival was probably an Osiris festival, and hence the festival of Dionysos may have been identical with it, as the coincidence of the dates pre-supposes.

Aristides Rhetor, writing about 160 A.D., says that at this Egyptian festival the water of the Nile is drawn and stored in wine-jars, for at this season it is considered to be at its purest; and he remarks that with time it becomes sweeter, just as wine

[1] M. Murray, *Osireion*, p. 29.

matures; and Epiphanius, writing about two centuries later, says that the Egyptians and other races draw water on the occasion of this festival, and store it up, and that in certain places it does actually turn into wine. This belief corresponds exactly to the stories related of the festival of Dionysos, at which, in certain localities, the water likewise turned into wine;[1] and the connection of Jesus with Dionysos in men's minds is shown by the introduction into the Gospel story of the incident of the turning of water into wine at the marriage-feast at Cana, which miracle is commemorated by the Church each year on January 6th, the very date of this festival of Dionysos.

Now Clement of Alexandria, writing in the year 194 or thereabouts, says that the semi-Christian sect of Gnostics in Egypt, known as the Basilidans, celebrated this date and feasted thereon; and gradually we find the Christians of Syria and elsewhere adopting this day, January 6th, as the anniversary of the baptism of Jesus in the Jordan.

---

[1] Athenæus, bk. i. ch. 61; Pausanias, vi. 26; Pliny, *Hist. Nat.*, li. 106; xxxi. 13.

By the Fourth Century the custom was widespread, and at Antioch in the year 386 the two great Christian festivals are stated to have been Easter and Epiphany, the latter being held on January 6th, and being celebrated by the blessing of all rivers and springs, and by the drawing of water for use at baptisms throughout the year. This word "Epiphany" means in Greek the "Apparition" or "Manifestation" of a deity, for Christ was deemed to have manifested Himself first at His baptism in the Jordan; but since He was said to have performed at Cana the same miracle of turning water into wine performed annually by Dionysos on this date, and since this was the first manifestation of His miraculous powers, the word "Epiphany" gradually came to refer also to the Cana miracle, which was likewise commemorated on this great day.

Thus the Christian festival of the Epiphany, in so far as it commemorated the baptism, and the miracle of turning water into wine, was simply a perpetuation of the festival of Dionysos, with whom Jesus had in pagan eyes so much in common,

246

and the corresponding Nile-festival of Osiris. But there was another "manifestation" which gradually came to be celebrated at this same feast, namely the manifestation made to the Magi by means of the Star of Bethlehem at the time of the nativity of Jesus; and it is this aspect of the festival which has survived down to the present day, and is now the accepted *raison d'être* of Epiphany.

The story of the Magi is found only in the latest of the Synoptic Gospels, that of St. Matthew, where it is said that wise men—no definite number is given—were guided to Bethlehem by the miraculous star; but since the tale does not appear in the other Gospels, nor is there any reference to it in the other books of the New Testament, it must be regarded as a legend. Its origin, however, is entirely obscure, though the fact that the wise men were understood to be Magi, that is to say, Persian priests, suggests that the source of the story may have been some incident recorded in the now lost scriptures of the Persian god Mithra, whose worship was the great rival of Christianity. At the birth of Mithra the babe was adored by shepherds, who brought gifts to him, which incident seems to have been the origin of the tale of the shepherds adoring the infant Jesus given in St. Luke;[1] and therefore there is no reason why the story of the Magi should not also have been borrowed from Mithraism. Mithra's birthday was always celebrated on December 25th, the date afterwards adopted as the anniversary of the birth of Jesus; and if the legend of the Magi is Mithraic, it may be that these wise men were there said to have arrived at Mithra's cradle twelve days after the actual birth, that is to say, on January 6th. But this is a guess, and the reason why the coming of these Magi was assigned to this day is really quite obscure.

At any rate the Christian Epiphany came to be connected with this event certainly as early as the Fourth Century; and soon the legend had developed, so that the "wise men" of St. Matthew became three kings named Balthasar, Melchior, and Kaspar, to whom the first three days after New Year are sacred in the Roman Catholic

[1] Luke ii. 15, 17.

calendar, and whose supposed bones are now preserved as relics in the Cathedral of Cologne! It may be said in passing that the perpetuation of this obscure legend in the Anglican Prayer Book by the Collect and Gospel appointed to be read at the Epiphany is almost an outrage in the Twentieth Century. A man of education can hardly be expected still to make a holy day of the pagan feast of Dionysos, and to refer in his prayers to God's goodness in revealing His son's birth to these fairy-tale kings by means of the perfectly incredible antics of a star.

Cassian (360?–435) says[1] that in his time all the Egyptian provinces regarded the Epiphany as commemorating also the actual birth of Jesus, the date December 25th being not yet recognised; and there is evidence to show that January 6th was widely regarded in the East as the anniversary of His nativity. This may perhaps have been due to the fact that our Lord was thought to have been exactly thirty years of age at His baptism, though the Gospel of St. Luke is not so precise,[2]

[1] Cassian, *Collat.*, x. 2.    [2] Luke iii. 23.

and hence that the one date covered the two events. It was the custom of the royal house in Egypt to celebrate what was called the *Sed*-festival at the completion of a period of exactly thirty years from the calendar date, whatever it might be, at which the Pharaoh, before he succeeded to the crown, had been chosen or appointed by his father as the future sovereign. This word *sed* means "to open" or "to expose,"‚or perhaps "to make manifest," and was the name of a god later identified with the god Wepwet, "The Opener of the Ways," or "Guide," who figured conspicuously in the ceremonies. At this festival the Pharaoh was made manifest as an incarnation of Osiris, and hence there may have been some tradition that Osiris was incarnated or chosen to be Lord of mankind exactly thirty years before he attained his earthly throne as Pharaoh. Osiris and Dionysos being identified, the idea perhaps passed thus into Christian minds that the manifestation of Jesus at His baptism occurred, like a Pharaoh's *Sed*-festival, exactly thirty years after His divine appointment, or birth in this case, which would give point to the remark of Origen, quoted above, that Jesus was no mere Pharaoh to have his birthday celebrated. In this regard it is to be noted too, that Zoroaster, the old Persian law-giver, is said to have been inspired by the Spirit of God, which descended upon him at the age of thirty.

Be this as it may, January 6th, the Epiphany, was for some generations the accepted anniversary of the Nativity, at the same time that it was the anniversary of the baptism, the miracle at Cana, and the coming of the Magi; and in the next chapter I will show how that date was abandoned in favour of December 25th.

# CHAPTER XXIII

## THE ORIGIN OF CHRISTMAS AND OTHER
## COMMEMORATIONS

IN the last chapter I pointed out that the day on
which Jesus was born was unknown, and that the
Christians at length selected January 6th as a
suitable date for the celebration of His birthday,
that da· having been chosen earlier as the anniversary of His baptism, the general feeling being
that the nativity and the baptism called for an
identical commemoration. There were other
dates, however, which were also thought by some
to mark His birthday: Clement of Alexandria,
for instance, writing towards the end of the Second
Century, says that he himself thinks He was born
in November, while other chronologists in Egypt
give the date as the 25th day of the month
Pachons, corresponding to a date in May, and yet
others prefer the 24th or 25th day of Pharmuthi,
which would be some time in April. Another

chronologist, in about the year 243, placed the birthday at March 28th. Yet in spite of these different opinions, January 6th was, as I say, the generally accepted date.

But towards the close of the Fourth Century the Church began to feel the need of celebrating a particular birthday festival apart from the commemoration of the baptism, for the purpose of counteracting the influence of the Manichæan heresy which declared that Jesus had been a phantasm and had never been born at all; and while the anniversary of the spiritual birth or "manifestation" was left at January 6th, in accordance with the dictum of Chrysostom and others that the divine life of Jesus had begun only at baptism, the anniversary of the Nativity, which was carefully distinguished as the birth "after the flesh," was changed to a new date, December 25th.

This new date, however, could hardly have been very convincing at first, for it was obviously chosen entirely under pagan influence, December 25th having been from time immemorial the birthday of the Sun, and celebrated as such with great rejoicings in many lands. The choice, in fact, seems to have been forced upon the Christians owing to the impossibility either of suppressing so ancient a custom or of preventing people from identifying the birth of Jesus with the birth of the sun; and it was necessary, therefore, to resort to the artifice so frequently employed and so openly admitted by the Church, namely, that of giving a Christian significance to an irrepressible pagan rite. A Christian Syrian writer of ancient times[1] definitely says that "the reason why the Fathers transferred the celebration from January 6th to December 25th was that it was the custom of the heathen to celebrate on the same December 25th the birthday of the sun, at which they lit lights in token of festivity, and in these rites and festivities the Christians also took part. Accordingly, when the doctors of the Church perceived that the Christians had a liking for this festival, they resolved that the true Nativity should be commemorated on that day."

[1] Quoted by Credner, "*De natalitiorum Christi origine*," in *Zeitsch. hist. Theol.*, iii. 2, 1833, p. 239.

# THE ORIGIN OF CHRISTMAS

The ancients had for untold ages mistakenly regarded December 25th as the winter solstice, instead of the correct date, December 21st; and even in the Julian calendar this error was perpetuated,[1] the 25th being termed the Day of the Nativity of the Sun, that is to say, the turn of the year after which the days would lengthen. But during the Third and Fourth Centuries Mithraism had gradually become the most important solar religion in the Roman Empire, the god Mithra being regularly styled "the Unconquerable Sun";[2] and thus we find that in the calendar of Philocalus, dating from A.D. 336, December 25th is marked *N. Invicti*, which stands for *Dies Natalis Solis Invicti*, "the Birthday of the Unconquerable Sun," the reference doubtless being to Mithra.

The first known reference to December 25th as being the birthday of Jesus occurs in a Latin work of about the year 354;[3] but here no festival is

---

[1] Pliny, *Nat. Hist.*, xviii. 221.
[2] Cumont, *Textes et Mons.*, i. 325.
[3] Mommsen, in *Abhandl. d. säch. Akad. d. Wissensch.*, 1850.

mentioned, and the date is only recorded as a piece of supposed history. The Emperor Honorius, however, who reigned in the West from 395 to 423, speaks of this date being kept in Rome as a new festival; and an imperial rescript of about the year 400 includes it as one of the three great feasts of the Church on which the theatres are to be closed, the other two being Epiphany and Easter. Its institution, it appears, was of Western origin, the worship of Mithra having been most powerful in the West; and gradually its observance moved eastwards. The Churches of Syria and Armenia, however, were horrified at the selection of such a date, it being the recognised date of the birthday of various pagan sun-gods; and they hotly accused the Western Church of sun-worship and idolatry, maintaining that January 6th was the more fitting date—forgetting, apparently, that January 6th was itself but the pagan feast of Dionysos and Osiris. They knew that Jesus was often spoken of as "the Sun,"[1] and that He was very nearly

[1] For instance, by Cyprian, *De orat. dom.*, 35, and by Ambrose, *Serm.*, vii. 13.

identified in pagan minds with Mithra; and they felt that the adoption of the sun's birthday as the birthday of Jesus was an unjustifiable admission of the power of heathendom. Augustine, also, begs his fellow-Christians not to regard the new date as sacred because of its connection with the sun, but on account of Him who made the sun.[1] Nevertheless, the Eastern Churches were forced in the end to acquiesce, and thus December 25th became established as Christmas Day. It did not become a *dies non* in the law-courts in Rome, however, until the year 534.

Now the winter solstice, as marking the beginning of the increase of the sun's power, was a far more important and joyous event in the north than it was in the warmer countries; and hence December 25th had always been celebrated amongst the Germanic and other northern races with far greater enthusiasm than it had been in the south and east, where the decline of the sun's strength was more pleasurable than the increase. Thus nothing so clearly shows that Christmas was

---

[1] Augustine, *Serm.*, cxc. 1.

a sun-festival as the fact that northern races to this day make a merrier holiday of it than do the southern peoples. To us it is still the turn of the year, after which we begin to think of the coming of Spring and the lengthening of the days.

The Venerable Bede,[1] writing in the early part of the Eighth Century, says that "the ancient people of the Anglian nation," by which he means the pagan English before their settlement in Britain round about A.D. 500, "began the year on December 25th, when we now celebrate the birthday of our Lord"; and he tells us that the night of December 24th-25th "which is the very night now so holy to us, was called in their tongue *Modranecht*, that is to say, 'Mothers' Night,' by reason of the ceremonies which in that night-long vigil they performed." He does not mention what those ceremonies were, but it is clear that they were connected with the birth of the sun-god. At the time when the English were converted to Christianity in the Sixth and Seventh Centuries the festival of the Nativity on December 25th had

[1] Bede, *De temp. rat.*, xiii.

been already long established in Rome as a solemn celebration; but in England its identification with the joyous old pagan Yule—a word apparently meaning a "jollification"—gave it a merry character which it did not possess in the south. This character has survived, and is in marked contrast to its nature amongst the Latin races, with whom the northern custom of feasting and giving Christmas presents was unknown until recent years.

The early Syrian writer quoted above states that there was an old pagan custom of kindling fires on December 25th, and that after the separation of Christmas from Epiphany these fires were kindled by Christians until the day of the latter festival, January 6th. These illuminations have survived in the burning of the Yule-log, and in the candles upon the Christmas-tree; and even down to present times it is considered correct to remove all Christmas decorations on, or before, January 6th (Twelfth Night). Possibly the Christmas-tree itself is derived from the tree hung with toys mentioned by Virgil as a feature of the

Saturnalia, the great Roman frolic which took place on December 17th, but which does not seem itself to have any clear connection with the Christmas festivity.

Our Christmas, then, is not, and in ancient times never was thought to be, the anniversary of the birth of our Lord: it is the birthday of the sun, and of Mithra in particular, and nearly everything about it is purely pagan.  But since the birthday of Jesus is to be regarded as the most important event in the world's history, and since its actual date is unknown, it is fitting that its commemoration should perpetuate a happy festival of immemorial antiquity; and we may heartily agree with Pope Gregory who, in 601, wrote to Mellitus, his missionary in England, telling him not to stop such ancient pagan festivities, but to adapt them to the rites of the Church; only changing the reason of them from a heathen to a Christian impulse.[1]  The Puritans, as a matter of fact, attempted in 1644 to prevent by an English Act of Parliament all merrymaking on Christmas

[1] Bede, *Ecc. Hist.*, xxx.

Day, and they succeeded in killing the festival in Scotland; but in England the Act was repealed by Charles II, and the traditional gaiety of the day was restored.

In regard to Easter, I have already pointed out that since our Lord rose from the tomb on the Sunday after the Passover, and since the Passover was originally a Spring festival, the date of the Christian celebration of the event coincided with the date of the resurrection of pagan gods such as Attis, who were originally gods of vegetation, at the season of the Vernal Equinox. Amongst the Anglo-Saxons the month of April was dedicated to Eostre or Ostâra, Goddess of Spring; and her great feast has given its name to our Easter. Here again the Church was quite frank about it, and Bede states that the feast in England was simply "the old festival observed with the gladness of a new solemnity,"[1] while the ecclesiastical historian Socrates[2] says that it was in general a perpetuation of an older usage, "just as many other customs have been established."

[1] Bede, *De temp. rat.*, xv.  [2] Socrates, *Hist. Ecc.*, v. 22.

The Festival of St. George, celebrated by the Church on April 23rd, has been shown by Frazer[1] to have replaced the pagan festival of the Parilia, the "Birthday of Rome"; and I may add that St. George himself is none other than the Egyptian god Horus who speared and slew the monster typifying the evil deity, Set. The Festival of St. John the Baptist on June 24th has replaced the midsummer water-festival in honour of certain gods such as Adonis;[2] for the Church, being unable to stop the people rolling in the morning dew or bathing in the springs and rivers on that day as a safeguard against future misfortune, placed the occasion under the patronage of their saint of the waters, and so permitted the custom to be continued, thus perpetuating it in many countries to this very day. The Festival of the Assumption of the Virgin Mary, celebrated by the Roman Church on August 13th, is, as I have said elsewhere, no other than the festival of Diana. Lammas, on August 1st in the Church Calendar, is the

[1] Frazer, *The Magic Art*, vol. ii. ch. xix.
[2] Frazer, *Adonis, Attis, Osiris*, bk. i. ch. ix.

Anglo-Saxon *Hlafmæsse*, the "Bread Ceremony," an ancient pagan festival of thanksgiving for the ripening of the corn. The Festival of All Souls is the ancient Egyptian Feast of Lamps. The Fast of Lent perhaps perpetuates the forty nights of lamentation in the mysteries of Proserpine and other forty-day periods of mourning in primitive religions; though it is to be noted that the forty-day Lent only dates from about A.D. 600. The word "Lent" means simply "Spring," and there can be no doubt that it was in its primitive origin a period of rustic propitiation prior to blossom-time and the renewal of the earth's greenness at the Vernal Equinox which was so widely regarded in paganism as the annual season of the gods' resurrection.

# CHAPTER XXIV

## THE MISUNDERSTANDING OF CHRISTIANITY

A FACT which must be clear to those who have read the foregoing chapters is that Christianity developed into a religion in a lurid pagan environment which could not fail to have its inflence upon the new Faith. The minds of its theologians, indeed, were saturated with the ideas of heathendom; and the doctrines and rites formulated by them show clearly both the vivid hues of the sacred carnivals of remote Antiquity, and the stains of that dark and fearful welter of primitive superstition amidst which the religion was nursed. The blood and wine of ancient sacraments are spattered across the very face of Christian theology, and its dogmas carry to this day the tell-tale marks of their inception amidst the barbaric splendours and the awful shambles of a forgotten age. Joy and terror mingle in the Church's liturgy; the triumphal shout of the old gods is

264

echoed in its festivals; and the groans of innumerable incarnate deities slain for the remission of sins are heard like an undertone in its prayers and its chantings.

Thus the Christian thinker of the politer Twentieth Century, in urging the necessity of the task of separating the pagan element from the basic truths of the Faith, must feel that no tinkering, such as is being conducted in England in regard to the Prayer Book, can be of much service. There must be a wholehearted movement back to the real Jesus and His teachings, so that Christianity may be understood to consist not in the adoration of the mystic crucifix, but in frank obedience to the historic Master, and service to God along the lines laid down by Him —in so far as we can trace those lines in such parts of our existing literary authorities as seem to be genuine. It must be candidly recognised that the old interpretation of Christianity is faulty; and just as our forefathers discarded such earlier doctrines as the Ransom Theory, so we must be prepared to abandon other dogmas unworthy of this age, however deeply custom has made them seem to be involved in the orthodox creed.

Now, one of the most obvious facts in regard to the historic Jesus is that He had extremely little to say about the next world: practically the whole of His teaching was concerned with conditions in this life. It was mankind's rightness of thought and consequent happiness; it was the ideal state of society on earth developing in the sunshine of the love of God, with which He was concerned; and we cannot remind ourselves too often that the improvement of the affairs of this world, and not the defining of those of the next, was ever uppermost in His mind. He laid down certain spiritual principles, certain rules of conduct, by the observing of which the human heart might fit itself to receive here and now the blessings from on high. "Come unto me, all ye that labour and are heavy laden," He said, "and I will give you rest. Take my yoke upon you, and learn of me, and ye shall find rest unto your souls; for my yoke is easy and my burden is light."[1]

[1] Matt. xi. 28.

He delivered no dissertations upon the nature of God, or upon the composition of the Holy Trinity, or upon the vicarious sacrifice necessary to redemption, or upon the dependence of salvation upon certain sacraments; nor did He speak much about rites, ceremonies, and observances, except that He told His followers not to make a stupid sort of holy-day of the Sabbath, not to bother about outward forms, and not to make a show of their prayers. For Him ritual had no significance, and there were no theological dogmas to be recited: He knew no theology, indeed, beyond the fact that God is love and that the Kingdom of God in the hearts of men can and will be established on this earth by obedience to the rules He gave us by precept and example. The things He taught had been preached, in one part or another, by great thinkers of widely separated nations and eras; but never have they been put so clearly and forcibly as by Him, never have they been so knit together to constitute a ready guide to ordinary men, never have they been backed up by so fine an example of how one gallant individual can live for the good of others, never have they been so free from the teacher's own peculiar theology and eschatology.

But man is a craven creature at best, and in early times, beset as he was by haunting fears of the unknown, he was more ready to listen to the whispers of his inherited superstitions and to pacify with rites and ceremonies the terrible wrath of an imagined Heaven, than he was to follow so simple an example of trust in the goodness of God as that set by Jesus. Thus, in general, the ancient Christian writings, and, in particular, the Prayer Book still in use in England, may be said to palpitate with nervous uneasiness. "Spare us, good Lord, and be not angry with us for ever," groans the Litany; "From thy wrath, and from everlasting damnation, good Lord, deliver us!" The frightful old myth of the Flood is introduced into the Anglican prayers for fine weather, one of which begins with the ludicrous words: "O God, who for the sin of man didst once drown all the world except eight persons . . . ;" and a prayer in time of sickness reads: "O God, who in Thy wrath didst send a plague upon thine own people in the wilderness, and also didst slay with the plague of Pestilence threescore and ten thousand, have pity on us, that like as thou didst command the destroying Angel to cease from punishing, so it may please thee to withdraw from us this plague." The prayer for fine weather begins: "O God, who hast justly humbled us by thy late plague of immoderate rain . . . ;" and the prayer for rain speaks of "the scarcity which we do now most justly suffer for our iniquity."

It is the old pagan instinct within us which thus blasphemes, imputing to the God of Love the motives of a vindictive goblin. At the festival of the Innocents, celebrated by the Church on December 28th in commemoration of a massacre which pretty certainly never took place, God is termed the author of the supposed slaughter; for the Collect for the day begins with the shocking words: "O God, who madest infants to glorify thee by their deaths. . . ." In the Anglican Communion service we are urged to eat the body and drink the blood of Jesus with proper sentiments of piety, lest "we kindle God's wrath against us, and provoke him to plague us with divers diseases and sundry kinds of death." And all through the Book rings the frightened cry: "Spare us, good Lord; spare us, miserable sinners!"—while fawning words of adulation and flattery are poured out in the hope of pleasing the wrathful Being.

These, and the like, are the relics of heathendom which need to be removed from the Christian liturgy, so that religion may be headed in the direction in which our Lord intended it to move, namely, towards the Kingdom of Heaven on earth, and away from the supposed menace in the skies. The Christianity of Jesus Christ does not emphasise the wrath of God, or His infliction of punishment, but sees mainly His love, and His unlimited forgiveness of man's frailty. The supposed direct references of our Lord to hell-fire are all contained in the Gospel of St. Matthew, the latest and most unreliable of the Synoptics, and are not corroborated by the earlier records of His sayings;[1] while the "wrath of God" is only mentioned in an obvious editorial gloss in the late Gospel of St. John.[2] Indeed, the whole conception of a Place of Torment where the wicked shall be punished with physical pain, and of a wrathful God who is a sort of combined policeman, magistrate, gaoler, and executioner, cannot be traced to the thoughts of Jesus, but belongs to a primitive age, and is entirely unworthy of our modern intelligence. Goodness is its own reward and sin its own punishment, in that the one is "life," because it leads to a condition wherein contact with God is established, and the other is "death," because it leads to a condition wherein God is shut out. Hell, so far as one can interpret the teaching of Jesus, was simply the Outer Darkness, the exclusion from the Kingdom of God, a state of mind wherein that worm,[3] conscience, never rested and the fires of remorse were not quenched. He recognised a spirit-world; for Peter, who had

---

[1] The words in Mark ix. 43, 44, are allegorical; Cruden, *Concordance*, "*Worm.*"      [2] John iii. 36.
[3] Mark ix. 44, quoting from Isaiah lxvi. 24.

known Him and had listened to His teachings, believed that during those hours between His collapse upon the cross on the Friday evening and His appearance, alive, on the Sunday morning, He had preached to the spirits of the dead,[1] and it is to be presumed that this belief was based upon something which Jesus had said to that effect. But there is no place in our Lord's eschatology for the idea of eternal torture as the punishment of evil-doing, nor is it possible for the modern mind to conceive of an almighty and loving God as being at the same time a fiendish monster deaf to the piteous shrieks of the damned.

The eternal fire of Hell presided over by Satan is a pagan belief which attached itself to Christianity some time before the composition of the Gospel of St. Matthew, that is to say, after A.D. 100. The references of Jesus to Satan are so rare and so vague that one may suppose Him to have had no belief in a personal Devil,[2] though He

---

[1] 1 Peter iii. 19; iv. 6.
[2] The whole passage in Matt. xxv. 31–46 is of very dubious authenticity.

certainly believed in the powers of evil. The Christian idea of the Prince of Darkness seems to have entered the Faith through Mithraism, wherein Mithra was "Light" personified, and hence Evil was "Darkness"; and Satan is simply the old Persian Ahriman, the eternal enemy of Ormuzd, and the ancient Egyptian Set, the opponent of Osiris. In his form as Mephistopheles he is to be traced to the once much-loved god Pan; and as Beelzebub he is Zeus Myiagros, "the Disperser of the Flies," who, to the Philistines at Ekron, was *Ba'al-z'bub*, "Lord of the Flies," a once benevolent god, patron of the flocks.

Christianity has concerned itself so much with this mythical Devil, with the fiery furnace, and with man's escape from it through the atoning sacrifice of Jesus Christ upon the cross, and it has advocated so continually the worship of Jesus as God and Saviour, that it has detached the attention of its members from the fact that the mission of the Faith should really be the furtherance of the Kingdom of God on earth, the establishment of right conditions amongst living men. The

work of the Christian is work in this world un-
hampered by terrors about the next.   There is no
time to waste in kneeling in fear before an angry
Deity, in telling Him what a splendid God He is,
in imploring Him to do us no harm now or here-
after, in performing endless rites at His altars for
our safety: the churchman has a better thing than
that to do in church, namely, to pray for strength
to obey Christ instead of merely worshipping Him.
It is a Christian's business, by his thoughts and
actions in everyday life, to get on with the improvement of social conditions, so that that ideal state
of society, preached by Jesus, shall in due course
be brought into existence.   But this is not the
view of orthodoxy: in its opinion the chief object
of the Christian is the salvation of his own soul by
the practice of certain rites and ceremonies, and
by adherence to, and a repetition of, a belief in its
dogmas.   It is the baptismal water which marks
the redemption from sin; or it is the eating of the
body and the drinking of the blood of Jesus which
establishes communion with Him; or, again, it is
the rehearsal of the creed which is the sure defence

against hell-fire; and so forth. The statement is never made that the one and only hope for us lies not in ritual, nor in sacrament, nor in worship, but in the putting into practice of the teaching of Jesus Christ—that teaching which urged trust in the love of God, affection and consideration for one another, friendship for the socially impossible, the courage of one's convictions, the fearlessness of the consequences in doing what one believes to be right, the forgiveness of insults, benevolence towards one's enemies, the refusal to judge others, modesty, the avoidance of all wish to be well spoken of by the conventional,[1] the control of the tongue, the observance of law and order, the banishing of worries, and all the other precepts which make for concord here on earth.

The mistaken attitude of Christianity is very largely the fault of St. Paul, whose figure, like a cloud, intervenes between the Christian and the historic Jesus. Paul was not very interested in Christ the Teacher: he was more concerned with Christ the divine Human-Sacrifice. "The Greeks

[1] Luke vi. 26.

seek wisdom," he said with scorn, "but we preach Christ Crucified."[1] He did not want to think of Jesus the man: he preferred the ecstatic picture of the divine Christ. "Though we have known Christ after the flesh," he declared, "yet now henceforth know we him no more."[2] He even repudiated the idea that he had learnt the genuine teaching of Jesus as related by the disciples, for he said: "I neither received the Gospel of man, neither was I taught it, except by the revelation of Jesus Christ,"[3] meaning to say that his revelation of the sacrificial Lamb of God, slain for the remission of sins, was far more important than the observance of the rules laid down in our Lord's ministry. But in this Twentieth Century thoughtful men, like the Greeks of old, seek wisdom—that wisdom which shall promote the establishment on earth of the Kingdom of God; and the tendency amongst laymen is to turn always more and more towards that true and historic Jesus Christ who now can only be reached by pushing one's way,

[1] 1 Cor. i. 17–29.  [2] 2 Cor. v. 16.
[3] Gal. i. 12.

as I have attempted to do in these pages, through the phantom crowd of savage and blood-stained old gods who have come into the Church, and, by immemorial right, have demanded the worship of habit-bound man.

**THE END**

Printed in July 2022
by Rotomail Italia S.p.A., Vignate (MI) - Italy